Life's Lessons
and a
Butter Churn

Memories from Another Time, Another Place

By

Theresa Hanvey Fallwell

For Ruth
Theresa Fallwell
10/26/18

DEDICATION

For my precious family
Yesterday, Today, and Tomorrow

Gwen, Bryce, Abbey, and Claire
Patrick, Terri, Christie, Josh

TABLE OF CONTENTS

Foreword

FOREWORD

A frequent contributor to the Old Huntsville Magazine, Theresa has the ability to draw you into her stories and make you feel like you're actually there with her. You will find yourself in the kitchen with her grandmother; watching as she prepares fresh chicken for frying, making cornbread and beans. Recalling the days when families worked together, she brings to life the people she knew, the tender moments she experienced and even the injustices done by others. A gifted writer with the ability to recreate the terror of a tornado outbreak in Hurricane Valley in 1920, Theresa Fallwell's collection of stories glitter like jewels in the literary crown of Alabama authors.

—Cathey Carney, editor of Old Huntsville Magazine

UNCOMMON, COMMON MEN

Standing in the middle of a rusty railroad bridge high above the muddy Missouri River with the wind buffeting my face was the first time I realized what a truly remarkable man my grandfather was. As I steadied him against the brisk wind, he began a monologue that defied his almost seventy years and failing health. With fist raised in defiance to the very wind, he said, "We built this bridge here! This Sibley Bridge, the very one on which you are standing!"

Grandad was quiet for a few minutes after that, and his demeanor changed as he began talking about the construction. He explained that it was a single track, three spans through truss Whipple bridge of almost 4,000 feet in length. Chartered in the late 1880s, it was not completed until 1915. With ease of memory, he talked about the quantity of steel needed, the crews and their tasks, and the myriad of hardships they encountered in building this bridge. He recalled his crew by name and the towns from which they came and the boarding house where they all lived. Then Grandad became quiet again. He pointed to a sandbar in the dark, swirling waters below us and said, "That piece of sand changed me forever."

With tears in his eyes, he told me the story of how on a cold December day, his best friend's son, who was on his crew, slipped on the icy bridge and fell to his death on that sandbar.

Grandad dove into the icy water and retrieved the young man's body and delivered it to his parents in Topeka, Kansas. That event so impacted my grandad that he gave up railroad construction and returned home to farm.

Grandad grew up in Lincoln County, Tennessee, the son of a farmer. He was schooled by his mother and from an early age was apparently a gifted reader and problem solver. When he was just a young teen, he decided to make his way out West where opportunity abounded. He and a friend ran away to Indian Territory together. Grandad eventually joined up with a railroad construction crew. Given his quick mind, he moved up the ranks to become a foreman and essentially, an engineer. Most of his time was spent working for the Atchison, Topeka, and Santa Fe Railroad Line. His conversations were peppered with names such as Leavenworth, San Bernindo, and Cairo as just some of the places he had stayed from Missouri all the way to California. His adventures living in the cabooses and in the construction towns that sprang up around the rail sites had always been entertaining, but on that trip in 1957 I realized what he had to say was not just entertainment, but history. Maybe, at thirteen, it was my emerging maturity, or perhaps I truly listened for the first time, but I realized that I was in the company of a truly uncommon man, and I was to find out just how uncommon this man was before this trip was over.

My aunt, uncle, and I, along with grandad visited two of his old railroad buddies on this trip. I was enthralled listening to these three old men tell stories about working on the bridge gangs all across this country. They referred to my grandad as Toby, a nickname I had never heard before. In this amiable chatter, they recaptured their youth, courage, sense of adventure, work ethic, and the camaraderie that existed among them despite an absence of fifty years. As they laughed and told tales on each other, a vigor returned that might have been expected in younger men. Amongst all the names of old friends that popped up, one name, Harry, peppered their memories repeatedly. Little did I dream that the Harry they were talking about was none other than Harry

S. Truman, 33rd President of the United States, and perhaps the reason why my grandfather was such a staunch Democrat.

After our trip to Sibley Bridge, we went to the Truman Library in Independence, Missouri early one morning. Mr. Truman unexpectedly appeared, and he and Grandad shared a Masonic handshake. They acknowledged their life long membership in that organization. Mr. Truman addressed my grandfather as Toby and the two began talking. I stood there in awe that my grandfather knew a president and was conversing with him.

The conversation started off discussing Truman's job when he was a clerk/timekeeper for the Santa Fe, and the relationship they had at that time and the people they knew. He acknowledged the friends that we just visited. From there a discussion of Fort Sill, Oklahoma ensued where Truman trained for the Missouri National Guard. My grandfather and he shared Fort Sill associations because that was near my future grandmother's home, and sometimes railroad gangs stayed there. Following that, my grandfather discussed with Mr. Truman aspects of his life as a farmer as they tried to "dig a living out of the ground," quoting Truman's own words. Then, a detailed exchange ensued regarding the politics of Truman and that period of history. It sounded as if it came right out of my history book. My grandfather quoted Truman's stand on political actions such as the Taft-Hartley Act, Truman Doctrine, and the Marshall Plan, as well as the attempted assassinations. The conversation continued when Grandad quoted Truman's own words about assuming the Presidency after Roosevelt's death as a ". . . load of hay falling on you." Grandad referenced old age using the same analogy. At that point, Mr. Truman turned to me and asked if I had seen his daughter, Margaret's, piano in the museum, and did I play. He took my hand and lead me to the piano where he played a little tune and I did the same. Never in my life have I ever wished I had practiced more than at that moment.

Mr. Truman then noted that he had a meeting that required his attendance and exited. I stood transfixed watching this historic figure get into his black car and drive himself away, waving continuously. Grandad in his usual succinct manner said as Mr. Truman left, "There goes an uncommon, common man," and I realized I was standing next to another such man.

A MEDICAL RUSE

North Alabama, like the rest of the country, found themselves under the Volstead Act in 1919. This act was passed by Congress, despite President Wilson's veto, as a companion act to enforce the unpopular 18th Amendment to the U.S. Constitution, which prohibited the production, sale, and distribution of intoxicating liquors.

Temperance was a hot topic in the first decade of the 20th century. Various groups such as the Women's Christian Temperance League, American Temperance Society, and the Anti-Saloon League were promulgating a complete ban of alcohol. These groups marched and rallied against the sale of all liquors as debasing family life, negatively impacting children, and compromising the economy; issues they collectively defined as moral depravity. Their progressive reform platform was based on the belief that prohibiting alcohol would elevate morality. Sobriety by national legislation was their goal. Their efforts and the passing of the 18th amendment and the Volstead Act saw the country enter an unpopular time called Prohibition until the 21st amendment ended that era in 1933.

The enforcement responsibilities for the 18th Amendment and the Volstead Act were given to the Internal Revenue Service under the Prohibition Bureau. Clarity in the laws was woefully lacking, and the result was often overzealous or misguided application, leading to opportunities for dishonesty. During Prohibition, it was not illegal to consume alcohol. It was only the manufacture, sale, and transport of liquor that was illegal. Any amount of beer, wine, or spirits contained in the home was legal. Battles ensued over the ambiguous distinctions between consumption, possession, and property. Agents of the Prohibition Bureau became known as "reveneroos" and wielded almost unlimited power to confiscate, destroy, and arrest without due process of the law. Despite this ambiguity, Prohibition initially appeared successful as measured by a drop in consumption, fewer arrests for drunkenness, and a reduced price for product; however, as Mark Twain stated, "The more things are prohibited, the more popular they become."

The demise of Prohibition in 1933 came about primarily because of unintended consequences of the laws. First, illegal production of alcohol skyrocketed through the creation of a new industry, bootlegging, and its organized criminal component. The illegal products, white lightning or hooch, were manufactured without oversight which lead to health concerns, including poisonings. Secondly, the illegal alcohol was not taxed which meant a loss of government revenue. Third, a new cultural icon sprang up, the speakeasy, to provide liquor to patrons. These establishments were prosperous, but often associated with violence. Lastly, since Prohibition did not have public support and was considered an invasion of privacy, creative people found ways to circumvent the laws. Hollow canes, books, and flasks were the usual means that the general public used to sidestep the laws relative to transporting and consuming liquors outside private homes.

The laws, though poorly defined and difficult to enforce, did provide exceptions for medicinal purposes as identified by doctors, dentists, and veterinarians. Despite the fact a consensus of doctors found no validity in alcohol for treatment of diseases, the public supported this exception and provisions were made to accommodate prescriptions of *spiritus frumenti* or spirits of the grain. Prescription forms were printed so the number of prescriptions written by any doctor could be regulated by the government and, in some cases, the state. A prescription required identification of the spirit such as rye, scotch, or gin. Specific diseases for treatment were identified on the form and included diabetes, cancer, indigestion, depression, and toothache. Some twenty-seven diseases were registered in which alcohol could be prescribed legally. Even the quantity of alcohol filled by each pharmacy was tracked and bottles were embellished with labels like "Perfection for Medicinal Purposes." Daily doses were usually a tablespoon three times a day, and the maximum allowed per prescription was a pint. The cost for a pint was about $2.50 which would be equivalent to about $35.00-$40.00 today. Regardless of these regulations limiting or forbidding alcohol, one enterprising visitor to Huntsville found a creative way to get around the law.

A salesman named Coffey was making a marketing trip to Huntsville during Prohibition. After he finished his calls for the day it was too late to head out to the next town, so he decided to spend the night in Huntsville before moving on to Nashville in the morning. After dining, he retired to his room and wrote a note requesting some whiskey. He hired a boy to take the note and cash to the pharmacy before it closed. The little boy returned shortly telling the man that the pharmacist could not fill his request unless it was signed by a doctor according to the rules established by the amendment. The little boy in a halting manner tried to explain Prohibition to the salesman as the pharmacist had explained it to him. The salesman listened politely and asked for his note. After his name he wrote M.D. and sent the boy back to the pharmacy. The child returned with the requested whiskey and received a nice tip.

The following morning, the salesman stopped in at the pharmacy. Greeting the man, the druggist addressed him as Dr. Coffey. He asked him how his patient was doing. The salesman then told the druggist that he was not a doctor, but a salesman from Chicago. Surprised, the pharmacist questioned his note from the previous night in which he signed his name with a declaration of M.D. Mr. Coffey replied that the M.D. did not stand for medical doctor, but simply a statement of his condition, mighty dry. The druggist was left with some explaining to do to the alcohol regulators.

DRUNKEN COWS

Grandad always said he had seen many men falling down drunk in his years on railroad bridge gangs and in the shanty towns that sprang up throughout the west in the early 20th century. The liquor flowed. Fist fights and shootings were common. He was a teetotaler, but quickly learned to identify changes in behaviors that pointed to drunkenness in order to take evasive action. Staggering, slurring of words, loss of inhibition and other social and physical variations of behavior alerted him to potential problems related to alcohol consumption; however, he also noted that being familiar with drunk men did not necessarily prepare him for the encounter he had with his cows one day in early 1920.

My grandparents bought the farm where they lived all their lives in 1920. The two-story frame house with tin roof had three bedrooms, a parlor, kitchen, dining room, and enclosed sunroom. A front porch extended the width of the house and overlooked a huge apple orchard and the most beautiful valley imaginable. A dirt road provided necessary access. Approximately 90 acres comprised the farm with a third being mountain land and two thirds being arable land. A barn, smokehouse, chicken houses, shed, and other out buildings were in place. One good fresh well and two sulphur wells provided water. In other words, it was a perfect place to establish a home for a growing family and a farm to produce income.

The first thing Grandad did after buying the farm was to get animal stock in place. He bought two pigs, a sow and a boar. Chickens and milk cows were purchased as eggs and milk were staples immediately necessary. He also bought two mules, Dick and Dinah, for plowing come spring, and arrangements were made for cotton, corn, and wheat seeds.

Since the weather was too cold for planting, Grandad and Grandma decided it would be a good time to go back to his parent's home in Tennessee to get some items that had been donated to the new couple. A rocking chair, a wash stand, and a wardrobe would add to their meager furniture.

Being new to the area, Grandad asked around for recommendations for a hired hand to look after the farm and animals while they made the three-day trip to Tennessee. Mr. Elisha's name kept coming up in conversation. Grandad interviewed him and hired him for the job. He was to stay at the house, feed and water the animals, and generally oversee the place. With arrangements made, they took off for Tennessee early one morning.

Upon their return things on the farm looked fine. Mr. Elisha told him there were no problems and that he had walked the fence line every day. Grandad was a little suspicious as he smelled the tell-tale odor of alcohol but said nothing. Once the furniture was unpacked, Grandad headed to the barn to check on his animals. The mules and chickens were fine. He gathered a few eggs to take to Grandma. Next, he headed to the other side of the barn to see about his milk cows, but they were not in the barn. They must be in the pasture, but they were not there either. Grandad became concerned. Then he saw a break in the fence leading to the apple orchard. He had not, as of yet, dealt with the orchard since purchasing the farm. He knew pruning was needed and lots of spoiled apples were on the ground as the farm had been unoccupied for at least a year before they bought it. Suddenly, he spied his three milk cows. One was down on the ground, not moving, and two were staggering around consuming half-rotted apples like they were drunk.

Grandad knew immediately what happened. The cows entered the orchard through the break in the fence and feasted on the vast amount of fermented apples lying all over the ground. It had to have been a feeding frenzy. The dead one probably swallowed the apple whole, as a cow's oral structure is not very mobile and they have fewer teeth than many animals and do little chewing until the cud is brought up. Cow are ruminants as they have cloven hoofs, multiple stomachs, and chew their cud. This cow's esophagus was blocked, and she probably choked to death.

The two cows that were still alive were standing and consuming fermented apples as fast as they could pick them up. Grandad recalled that their heads were raised up toward the sky and swinging quickly back and forth. A soapy looking saliva was dripping from their mouths in long strings, and a look of pure ecstasy was on their faces. Their udders were distended, and the cows were bellowing. Additionally, they were bloated due to gas pressure in the stomach which the cows were unable to release. The sugar overload from the apples coupled with the sudden change in their diet apparently caused these drunk-like behaviors. Grandad did not attempt to milk the cows as he feared they would be unable to balance enough to stay on their feet and he didn't want to find himself under what he termed a drunken cow.

Despite the humor associated with the drunken cows, Grandad knew their lives were in danger. He had to get them away from the fermented apples or they would continue to gorge themselves and die. Tying a rope around each one's neck, he struggled with them, but finally drug them back to the well area behind the barn. There he got a rubber hose, buckets of water, and a large funnel. The cows were tied to a fence post and Grandad put the water hose in each cow's mouth. He poured copious amounts of water down their throats. The cows were already dehydrated so he thought it wouldn't hurt and the water might dislodge any obstructions and release the gas. The water worked; material from both ends evacuated and relieved them. The cows supposedly slept the inebriation off but continued hurting until they could be milked. Grandad was pleased that at least part of his investment was saved and they would have milk again.

Grandad told this story many, many times, and I never failed to laugh as he demonstrated the walk and actions of a drunk cow. He used the experience as a lesson to warn young people about the hazards of alcohol consumption, and about the importance of actually doing the work for which you are paid. Needless to say, the dead cow was buried and the orchard fence was repaired straight away; however, unfortunately both the fence and that beautiful apple orchard did not survive much longer due to the tornado that destroyed all of it later that spring.

TORNADO MONSTER OF 1920

Mention the word tornado in Alabama and you are likely to hear stories of miracles and devastation. Major outbreaks in 1965, 1974, and 2011 created a respect for weather that only those who live in a tornado prone area can appreciate.

Dark clouds, greenish skies, and warm, humid air propel the senses to a heightened state of anxiety. The television and radio stations, as well as the National Weather Center, become our collective eye on the sky with updates churning ever more rapidly as if in concert with the coming twister. Fear is enhanced if it is night time or the potential tornado is enshrouded in blinding rain. An overwhelming sense of vulnerability invades the mind and body as you rush around getting your kids, shoes, pillows in the tub or interior closet or in a cellar. With the media you can monitor your situation and assess your danger until all communication is lost. Then you are on your own to do battle with the monster.

Old people in Hurricane Valley talk about doing battle with their own monster. It was April 1920, a warm day according to my grandma. She had been in the garden all day planting onion shoots and preparing beds for the pepper seedlings she had growing in eggshell halves on the window sill of the sunporch. She had not planted them yet because she knew a killing frost was still possible. On her way back from the garden with my infant mother on her back, she wandered through the apple and peach orchards inspecting and enjoying the blooms and sweet aroma. The prospect for bumper crops this year were great, and she said a quick prayer hoping to ward off a late freeze.

Coming out of the orchards, Grandma became aware of a bank of dark clouds building off to the west. The breeze she enjoyed all day was gone and, instead, there was a foreboding stillness in the air which bothered her. After a quick supper of cornbread and milk, she and Grandad talked about the changing weather. Since Grandma grew up in Oklahoma she was all too familiar with twisters, cyclones, and dust devils. She did not use the word tornado, but instead, hurricane, as that was the term for such storms in the South at that time. It unnerved her that the place to which they moved was named Hurricane Valley indicating the propensity and frequency for such storms. As night approached, Grandma began to pace as she ascertained, without the help of meteorologists or media, that the weather was deteriorating. Grandad calmed her fears and they went to bed as the sun went down, but she insisted they sleep in their clothes.

Sometime during the night, they were awakened by a terrible noise. Grandma knew instantly what was happening. She grabbed my mother, who was sleeping with them, and jumped out of bed trying to find her shoes. Grandad did the same and quickly escorted them outside and down into the opening under the house which served as a root cellar and canned goods storage. They crawled deep into the recess where the clearance from the floor was only a few inches, but it was surrounded by a thick rock foundation. Strings of onions hanging from floor joists slapped them on the head as they moved toward the back. Potatoes and turnips concealed and protected by loose hay created a bumpy path. At the very back of the opening there were huge rocks that formed the back foundation of the house, Grandad positioned Grandma and the baby beneath him. It was damp. Thunder ricocheted off the mountains with a terrifying noise, and the lighting was so bad that the glow penetrated the cellar. The old, two story clapboard house started to shake and the windows rattled. Timbers split and old growth trees went down with loud cracks as the tornado approached. They were no match for the ferocious wind. Suddenly, the house above them seem to rise and fresh air came rushing in from somewhere. The noise was thunderous and came in waves. It would get quiet for a while and then it sounded as if another storm passed over. They stayed under the house for a long time. Finally, the noise ceased. Grandad tried to open the cellar door but found it impossible to budge. With no moon or other light to help him, he could not safely exit the area. Waiting till daylight seemed prudent. Lying there in the dark, they kept hearing a strange sound even after it was obvious that the storms had passed. The noise was fairly constant, and they thought it might have been trees coming down in the mountain behind them or possibly rain or hail.

With first light, Grandad found a way out of the cellar through pieces of tin, lumber, and trees. He made a path through the debris for Grandma. By now the baby was hungry and crying, so he made his way over to the old sulfur well where jars of milk were kept cold as there was no other refrigeration. I understand that was the day my mom gave up the bottle.

Grandad surveyed the damage in the dim morning light. The house was constructed with an L, housing a kitchen and dining area which stood directly over the part of the cellar where they had taken refuge. The huge rainwater silo attached there was also split into sections and scattered all over the farm. The main part of the house remained mostly intact, but with significant damage. The entire apple and peach orchards across from the house were completely gone except for one gnarled old apple tree which continued to live for another sixty years.

Grandad got his family safely into what remained of the house then set off on his mule, Dinah, to see about his neighbors. Fortunately, he found no real injuries, but major damage to houses, barns, and outbuildings. Other neighborhoods were not so fortunate as many people were injured or killed.

While Grandad was surveying the neighborhood, Grandma kept hearing that strange noise. In the dim light she could not determine where it was coming from or even what it was. At mid-morning Grandad returned and immediately saw the source of the noise. His newly purchased, prize bull was stranded in the fork of a huge hickory tree bellowing. Now Grandad had a dilemma. There was no way the bull could get down on its own. Should he shoot the bull and put him out of his misery, incur financial loss, and still have to get him down, or should he try to get him down alive?

The answer came when a county commissioner surveying tornado damage saw the bull in the tree and offered a suggestion as to how to get him down. He had seen a new piece of equipment that he called an earth mover with a bucket parked on a flatbed at the railroad depot. Perhaps the bucket would extend high enough and could be angled just right to collect the bull. He proposed severing the limb containing the fork right where it left the trunk. The forked part of the limb and the bull were about ten feet away from the trunk of the tree. If they could contain the bull in the fork and lower him slowly, the bull would probably survive. Someone would have to climb up that main limb to sever it.

Grandad liked the idea; anything to save his investment, so he and the commissioner left for town immediately. Since grandad was an old railroad man he knew everyone at the station and was certain he could make the necessary arrangements to borrow the earth mover. Sure enough the two of them were successful and they made their way back to Hurricane Valley late that evening. On the way they gathered a large entourage of onlookers on mules, horses and walking. Most had never seen such a piece of machinery.

Arriving at the farm, several men contributed ideas as to how to position the earth mover so that the bull's weigh would not cause it to topple. With kerosene lanterns for light, men positioned the contraption and found rocks to scotch the wheels to inhibit slippage. Grandad and a volunteer rode the bucket up the tree to position themselves on either side of the limb containing the fork. Fortunately, it was not too far up the tree to that limb. By now, the bull had stopped bellowing and was still.

Using a crosscut saw, the men started cutting the limb. Grandad always said he got the wrong end of that deal as the bull was facing outward and he had to watch for kicking legs and other unpleasant stuff. The men wielded the crosscut saw slowly and the limb began to show signs of the effort. Crack, creak the limb was beginning to separate. Suddenly, the weight of the bull and the crack in the limb caused it to descend slowly. The two men cutting the limb found refuge on the backside of the tree as the branch and bull came down perfectly in the bucket which they immediately lowered. The bull ended upright and escaped the fork by jumping out of the bucket. After escaping, the bull first appeared too traumatized to move. Someone threw a handful of hay at him; he jumped and started running as did the whole crowd surrounding the bucket. The bull did not appear physically hurt as he trotted off toward the barn. Grandad said even though that bull was saved, he never really fulfilled the purpose for which he had been purchased, but his adventure was the subject of much talk in the community.

Eventually the debris was cleared, the house repaired, and the old hickory tree grew stronger than ever. The orchard was turned to pasture, and the monster tornado of 1920 was relegated mostly to oral history. The story of the bull was good for a few laughs then, and even today. When the Hurricane Valley old-timers tell this story, it is still with a sense of relief that they survived this 1920 monster, and yet, they know there will be another monster and another battle someday as tornadoes are a way of life there.

Research into this violent tornado outbreak confirmed much of what I was told by family members and Hurricane Valley old-timers. The outbreak occurred over a three-day period near the end of April 1920. Scientists assessing records believe there were six F4 tornadoes and one F5 that night. There were also reports of numerous smaller tornadoes occurring throughout the area associated with that same front. Deaths from the violent outbreak included 97 in Alabama and 126 in Mississippi. These tornadoes were described as rapidly rotating and long-tracking.

Witnesses further stated that parts of north Alabama were swept clean with huge trees snapped and impaled into cliffs. Although it is impossible to identify the tornado that hit Hurricane Valley that night so long ago, the long path of the one that started at the junction of Morgan and Madison counties is a likely candidate. Until recently, the 1920 outbreak was listed as the third deadliest in Alabama history tying with the Palm Sunday outbreak of 1965. More recent outbreaks may have altered that ranking.

SANGIN' ON THE TATER KNOB

In the early 1900s, Tater Knob, a part of the lower Appalachian Mountains bordering Alabama and Tennessee, was an especially lush, green, mostly uninhabited deciduous forest filled with fresh water springs and cool glades that supported the slow growth of a medicinal herb, ginseng. This herb thrived within this setting due the vast and varied understory of plants, a rich, organic composition to the soil, the right amount of rainfall, a canopy of leaves for protection, and a well-defined cold season for dormancy.

Documented trade in ginseng can be traced back to the 1700s in this country, but some estimates suggest it goes back thousands of years. The Cherokees, who lived in the Appalachians, called this human shaped herb, manroot, and evidence exists for its use as currency as well as for its curative purposes. Ginseng hunting, or as it's known colloquially, sangin,' has been a tradition handed down from father to son for generations in the mountainous regions of this country. Even names synonymous with early pioneer life here, as well as the founding fathers, were associated with ginseng trade. China has always been a main importer of dried ginseng roots as they were valued for medical conditions including immune system disorders, aging, illness, appetite problems, insomnia, infection, sexual dysfunction, and nervous system problems, or even as a topical ointment, just to name a few. The herb can be used in tea, capsules, or extract. Such uses have truly made this extremely popular herb a cash crop for the ages.

The ginseng plant features a whorl of dark green leaves in three to five prongs coming from a stem. The number of prongs is dependent on the plant's maturity. In the early summer, plants produce small greenish blooms that extend directly from the whorls and in the fall, leaves yellow and red berries appear. To be worthy of harvest, plants should have at least three prongs, meaning the plant's age is probably three years. Also, for identification purposes, the ginseng plants tend to spread out horizontally to the ground. Roots are the treasure. They are oval shaped and tannish in color. The main root resembles the figure of a man. Long stringy roots emanating from the main root approximate human appendages.

September was usually the beginning of ginseng season for the hunters, and it was also the time we expected to see Lucas and Ernie. These two sangers regularly stopped by my grandparent's farm. They told tales of ginseng hunting to my Grandad and he allowed them to hunt on his property; perhaps because Grandad knew Ernie's sad story.

Ernie and his dad migrated to the area in 1914. Unfortunately, Ernie's father died shortly after arriving due to meningitis. Grandad found the 13-year-old boy sleeping in his barn one cold winter night and brought him home and fed him. With no social programs in place to care for this orphan, only the generosity of neighbors and the young boy's own resourcefulness kept him from starving. Ernie worked long, hard hours for his age. He plowed, planted, chopped, and picked cotton. He cut cedar posts for fencing, gathered and sold wild berries, grew vegetables, and hunted ginseng. He was no one's boy, and yet, everyone's boy.

Lucas was an old recluse living in a dilapidated log cabin near Cadillac Spring. He was compassionate toward Ernie and taught him mountain skills such as trapping, hunting, and gardening. These two set up a thriving, mutually beneficial ginseng business.

When sangin' season arrived, Ernie would hike to Lucas' cabin. The next morning the two guys would set a trotline in the creek, and begin their search for ginseng. First, they would visit the old, familiar sites which produced ginseng every year. In fact, they would visit any site that had ever produced ginseng. Lucas said you never could destroy a patch with careful harvesting. It might lay dormant for a long period of time, but it would come back. The most productive sites were on the north side of the mountain where the deep glades and rich woods held the moisture longer. Ernie always said Lucas could spot a plant half a mile away. Its berries, red and clustered and similar to a dogwood tree, gave it away. Lucas always cautioned for clear identification in case poison ivy also grew there.

When a patch of plants was found, Ernie and Lucas would yell loudly and sometimes fire off a pistol just for fun. Then squatting, they would pull out their knives and begin the process of extracting the gnarled, henna or ochre colored roots carefully from the ground to avoid breaking off any tendrils. The bigger the root, the happier they were and the louder they yelled. Roots were then placed in a heavy canvas bag which Lucas carried on his shoulder. There was always much discussion as to the size and shape of the roots. After harvesting the area, they planted the red berries to ensure that the patch would survive.

Sometimes the two guys would spend all day at one site, but usually they walked many, many miles searching for ginseng. It was not an easy task, walking up and down mountains, jumping eroded rivulet's, and fighting the thick vegetation. If they saw a squirrel or rabbit they might shoot it to cook over an open fire for supper. With quick wit, Lucas always said the only real drawbacks to sangin' were the chiggers, ticks, briars, snakes, and his bad knees.

Late in the afternoon, Lucas and Ernie would return to the Cadillac Spring cabin where they would prepare their supper of fish, squirrel, rabbit, or even turkey. The evening would pass with them reviewing their efforts, telling stories, singing, and whittling.

Lucas, with his infectious laugh always said, "We sang some and we found some 'sang and we ate some food. Guess we are livin' like kings."

Down from the mountain to the farm, the two of them would come after their season with their crop of ginseng swinging in the bag. They always shared stories of their good fortune with Grandad and told tall tales of their encounters with snakes or bobcats or other wild critters. They also would tell Grandad if anyone was using his mountain land for stills, poaching, or timber. It was also common for them to bring Grandma some wild pears to make jam. Lucas and Ernie, sitting on the front porch with their tea glass in hand, telling their stories would break into song.

Up in the morning, feelin' strong and stout,
Goin' over the mountain to catch some trout.
There's a great, big fog and a soakin' rain,
I'm on my way to Cadillac Spring.
Gonna climb them bushes, go over them rocks,
Making my way to the Tater Knob top.
A little ole squirrel and corn on the cob.
Goin' go sanin' on Tater Knob.

Next, the two men had to dry their ginseng before they could sell it to marketers in Tennessee. Prices varied by dealer, but they were happy if they received $45.00 a pound. That little extra cash helped pay the bills, but the best part was the friendship shared by the hapless child and the old recluse, and the genuine fun they had sangin'.

A resurgence in the ginseng trade has been fueled by a TV show and, also, by an amazing increase in the selling price. The latest estimate for ginseng was between five and six hundred dollars a pound, which makes it a very lucrative crop if it can be found. Hunters today face many more problems than Lucas and Ernie. Property rights, seasons, quantities, plant extinction, poaching, and an increased number of hunters all figure into the process. I can't help but wonder if today's hunters have as much fun as Lucas and Ernie did.

WESTERN NIGHT OPERETTA

For entertainment in the 1920s until the 1950s, schools often presented operettas. The term operetta had its origin in Europe and generally meant a genre of refined musical amusement lighter than an opera. Schools redefined the term to include dancing, singing, and various forms of artistic performance under a central theme. Most were held on a Saturday night and lasted, with intermission, about two hours. Parents often served cookies and punch, and each operetta was a major social event for the community. Young children and girls especially liked the operettas. Older boys were more hesitant to perform these "sissy" activities, so they often begged off because of chores or they simply did not show up on the night of the performance. To counter this attitude on the part of older boys, some were coerced into participation by proud parents. This is the story of how one of those reticent boys, Tommie, fought against such parental coercion and won his battle not to participate in the operetta.

The Western Night Operetta in May of 1922 was promoted as outstanding entertainment. There was to be square dancing, animal costumes, songs, a play, and a special reading from the *Illiterate Digest* featuring Will Rogers' political *humor* complete with his rope tricks. In addition, several children were to read their original poems, and solos on the piano, violin, and guitar were also scheduled. Costumes complimented the western theme with the girls wearing colorful, long crepe paper circle skirts that swayed as they danced and sang and big, paper flowers in their hair. The boys wore jeans with vests, cowboy hats, bandanas, and as many toy guns or knives as they could find. All this entertainment was set against an impressive stage backdrop of a broken-down fence appointed with bushes, sapling trees, and a big yellow, paper moon. Much time and effort had been spent to make Western Night Operetta the best ever.

At the time of the Western Night Operetta Tommie was eight years old. His part in the performance was as a dancer in the hoedown and a violin solo. His mother, a refined lady and a talented musician who played several instruments by ear, insisted he play the violin from an early age. The violin teacher lived across the football field from the school. So, once a week for three years on lesson day he would have to dress up in his Sunday clothes so that he would be properly attired to approach such a cultured instrument and walk across the football field to his teacher's house. An audience of older boys would lie in wait for him, laughing and calling him the "mowsician." The boy took great offense at this weekly teasing and dreaded the operetta because he knew it would only increase the harassment. He made many excuses to escape performing in the operetta, but his mother was insistent, thinking he had more talent than he did. When the program for the Western Operetta Night was finalized, he noted that his dance performance, which he wanted to do, was scheduled in the first act followed by the violin solo, which he did not want to do, in the second act. He began to develop a plan that would allow him to escape potential humiliation and future teasing by the older boys, and yet, not openly defy his beloved mother.

The first act of the operetta was quite entertaining for the large crowd that had gathered. The hoedown was well-received by the audience. The Will Rogers' act was a great hit as it was current with its political jokes and satire. Next, the primary children dressed as farm animals and did their little play and sang songs. Two piano solos later, intermission was announced. The performers and the audience all adjourned to the picnic areas under the big oak trees in front of the school for cool refreshments.

Amidst all the partaking of punch and cookies, Tommie slipped back into the auditorium unnoticed. From his violin case he pulled out a very large can of black pepper which he sprinkled all across the worn, wooden floor of the stage under cover of the stage curtain. After he disposed of the empty can, he quietly rejoined the others at the refreshment tables.

After intermission, the performers and the audience filed back into the auditorium. The first act, a lively dance number, was to be performed by the sixth-grade girls. The music began, and the girls started moving rapidly on the stage, bowing to partners, circling, and promenading home. Their long, crepe paper skirts grazed the floor with each bow and turn. Suddenly, one of the girls began sneezing uncontrollably, then another and another. Soon all the girls were sneezing so hard that their eyes were watering and their noses running. The dance movements were lost as they bumped into each other because they couldn't see, and some even fell as the floor became slick from all that moisture. Initially, subtle giggles from the audience turned into hysterical laughter as the situation deteriorated. The girls started crying because of the embarrassment. Seeking relief, they wiped their eyes and noses on the paper skirts which, of course, began to tear apart adding to their overall distress.

To this scene, add a distraught teacher running around dabbing at eyes with her handkerchief and trying to salvage skirts and modesty until she, too, was overcome with sneezing. Observers noticed what appeared to be dust clouds rising from the stage floor. Parents, with handkerchiefs in hand, retrieved their crying, sniveling children and headed home fussing about the lack of cleanliness and preparation of the stage for the operetta. It was with a sense of utter disbelief that the principal canceled the remainder of the operetta.

With a smug smile and a guilty sense of accomplishment,

Tommie took his violin home and somehow, never played another note. And, even though Tommie didn't know it, his mother was terminally ill by this time, and, of necessity, she relinquished her dream of him ever becoming an accomplished violinist. His means of escaping the operetta remained a secret until he confessed much later in life and at a considerable distance from his school. It might also be noted that for a number of years after the disastrous Western Night Operetta, the stage received particular attention and a personal inspection by the principal prior to any school function.

"GREAT AWAKENING"

The word revival in the South of the 1920s conjures up a plethora of images, an impressive culture of great religious awakenings in a variety of settings. From brush-arbors to camp meetings to tents or church buildings, these regularly scheduled awakenings focused on personal spiritual growth and a fervent relationship with God or rebuilding the church body following a lull or "backslide" in Christian enthusiasm or dedication. To the reverberating strains of "I'll Fly Away," or "Washed in the Blood," or "Land *Where* We'll Never Grow Old," generations of people dealt with the seductive influence of sins such as spirituous liquors, smoking, card-playing, dancing, gambling, and profanity. Revival entities had similarities, as well as individual differences by denomination and/or location. Commonalities included soul-saving preaching, congregational singing, testimonies, and altar calls. Some also had foot-washings, healing crusades, and Jericho marches. Most were held on summer nights and lasted from three days to two weeks.

Country churches replaced brush arbors, camp meetings, and tents as revival sites when electricity became more widely available. The novelty of electric lights and fans appealed to most attendants and promised to make the event more comfortable. Air conditioning was not yet available, and those open windows gave entry to all kinds of bugs, particularly moths attracted to the lights. Regardless of the conditions, revivals in the South were an important part of the culture, a means of attending to the spiritual needs of the community.

It was just such a revival setting in a church near New Market, Alabama, Rice's Chapel, that my late father had his own rather unique "great awakening." Old time, biblically focused religion was preached at Rice's Chapel both on Sundays and during this summer revival of 1929. The revival had been going on for several nights in extreme heat and humidity with capacity crowds. Hand fans advertising politicians and morticians were scattered on the wooden pews. Ladies claimed these fans and had them moving at breakneck speed trying to keep overheated, irritable babies from crying. All the church windows were flung open with men perched on the window sills to gain access to any possible breeze, and the hum of several new electric fans sounded like a swarm of insects. And still it was hot; just like hell was the analogy the preacher made as he extolled sinners to leave their lives of sin behind and accept Jesus Christ as personal Savior.

The itinerant preacher for the revival was a very tall, impressive man who moved about the church in an extremely animated fashion as he preached. The pulpit was rarely used because he wanted to be close to his congregation. He was known to stop mid-sentence and stare intently into someone's eyes as if singling them out for a sin. As the evening wore on and his passion grew, he gesticulated wildly with long arms circling high over his head to drive a point home. He was also possessed of a loud, deep voice that commanded attention, scared children, and required regular, congregational "amens!"

Coincidently, it was during this revival season that the church's oil lamps were replaced by those new-fangled electric lights. Two lights had been added to the sanctuary, one near the front and one near the back. Both lights hung low on long cords to place the illumination closer to the congregation for ease in reading their Bibles. The location of the lights had never been a problem until this preacher stepped out of the pulpit to preach. His animated style resulted in frequent collisions between his head or hands and the bare light bulb. The first night of the revival, my dad and the other teenage boys snickered every time the preacher banged into the light near the front of the church, disrupting the moths circling there. They dared not laugh out loud, but a stern look from the preacher warned them their indiscretions had not gone unnoticed.

The next night of the revival the preacher was expounding from the text of Deuteronomy and Exodus on God's provision of all our needs, specifically the story of the Israelites, manna, and the journey through the desert to Canaan. Gesturing toward heaven to indicate the source of the manna, this low hung light with it cadre of moths was causing too much of a distraction. After bouncing the light off of his head a couple of times and flicking moths away from his face and mouth, it was apparent that the serious nature of his message was being compromised by the comedy of him hitting the light. As a man prone to decisive action, he looked over at the young people sitting in the choir section and asked the boys to tie a knot in the long cord to raise the light. Well, my dad, being long and lanky, volunteered for this assignment. It was later he admitted that he really volunteered to impress a certain pretty young girl.

Young Ralph scrambled up to balance on the top of the back of the pew located right in the center front of the church. Using a long-handled broom that someone brought him, he reached over three feet or so and caught the electric cord with the light attached. He pulled it toward him and with great fanfare over the heat of the bulb, he tied a big, floppy knot in the cord. He then let the light swing back toward the preacher who measured the new height against his head and then against his up stretched hand. Seeing that the light still did not completely clear his hand, he asked Ralph to tie the light up just a little higher. Once again Ralph climbed to the back of the pew, and as he did he gave a quick glance to see if any of that bevy of pretty young girls in the choir loft was looking. He flashed them his best smile and with great drama, he stretched his arms and the broom way up over his head to catch the light cord for the second time. Against a backdrop of positive congregational comments about what a fine young man Ralph was despite the death of his mother, and a number of "atta boys," suddenly, an ear-splitting sound instantly silenced the congregation. An unloaded pistol that Ralph had stashed in the back of his pants under his shirt slipped out of the waistband and down his pant leg to the floor. When the pistol hit the ground from that height it sounded like a bomb going off.

Everyone froze with their eyes riveted on that shiny, silver revolver as it spun around and around and around. When the gun finally stopped spinning, one of the deacons calmly stood up, stepped in front of the preacher who was standing there in unaccustomed speechlessness, and retrieved the gun. Ralph climbed down from the pew, and the deacon handed him the gun. He took the gun in hand and dropped his arm to his side. Without a word, he turned around and slunk out of Rice's Chapel, but in the just breaking quiet he heard a child's rather sweet voice question, "Was that manna from heaven?"

As Ralph walked away from Rice's Chapel that fateful evening, he heard on the night air a single, spontaneous voice begin singing: "What can wash away my sins? Nothing but the blood of Jesus!"

Slowly, more voices joined in the singing until the night was absolutely filled with this musical indictment of him. Ralph heard the strains of that old familiar hymn, ironically his mother's favorite, as he retreated from his embarrassment, bad judgment, and perhaps, even a negative direction in his life into his own personal "great awakening." By the time he got back to his empty home that night he had judged his own behavior according to how his beloved mother would have if she had been alive. He knew she would have told him that the Lord's house is no place for guns even if bullies were lying in wait for you. She would have told him to find a better way to deal with such threats. She would have simply said that she expected better of him.

Although Ralph never went back to Rice's Chapel, he carried that old hymn with him for the rest of his life of 86 years, a sort of personal soundtrack which he often whistled when he was visiting the past in his mind. And, despite his "great awakening," at Rice's Chapel in 1929, he remained a colorful character who did get into mischief occasionally, but never any real trouble. His mother's faith in God, though she was absent from his life, remained his guiding influence on acceptable behavior. She would have been very proud of the good man he became and of the good life he lived.

BUSTER'S GHOST

It was a real shame one of the men gathered on the front porch said. Buster was a good man and shouldn't have died that way. That old horse of his was known to be aggravating. He would turn in a minute and bite your hand if you were brushing him or trying to put the bit in his mouth. They recalled he was a real kicker too, but never kicked Buster like that before. It was a bad blow to the head and knocked Buster out colder than a cucumber. His wife tried to wake him, but he was dead to the world. At the hospital, the doctors said he probably bled into his brain. His face was black and blue and both eyes were closed. Take him home and pray was all the doctors could offer. So they took Buster home and he died a few days later as did that aggravating horse, though not accidentally.

The funeral was a sad affair with lots of people in the community lamenting Buster's tragic fate. A group of his friends and family, led by Clyde, dug his grave. It took all day. He was buried in the cemetery behind the church. The cemetery was small, overgrown, and showing its age as evidenced by gravestones off kilter due to settling of dirt, but the sites were free and that was the custom.

Following the funeral, the same men covered the grave, and went back to Buster's house for the wake to support the family. As was the Southern custom in the 1930s, women were inside preparing food for the wake, and the men sat outside, usually whittling pieces of wood and sharing stories about the deceased. Food was served and evening came on.

Buster's friends moved to an area under a big oak tree as the women were busy cleaning up and getting kids ready to bed down on pallets. It was not unusual for mourners to spend the night at the deceased's house due to poor roads and the difficulties travelling at night.

As the men sat under the oak tree smoking and drinking in the semi darkness, the stories became less about the deceased and more about fishing, hunting, and moonshine. The late autumn air turned chilly just as the stories became scarier and more boastful. One man told, in gory detail, about the lovers who were mutilated over at a fishing spot near the Tennessee River. Another told of hearing an old owl hoot three times and wondered who would die next. Still another told of a scary encounter with a sheriff who got too close to his bootlegging operation and how he dodged buckshot, but his dog did not. Talk of ghosts, ghouls, and unexplained phenomena continued. Each man's story was more unnerving than the previous one.

Clyde suddenly stopped whittling his long, sharp stick and enthusiastically stated that he wasn't "no feared of ghosts." Several men admonished him not to tempt fate using their personal experiences with ghosts and haunts. One told how he should never go by Billing's Hollow at night as there is an old haunt that will scare you gray headed. It happened to his cousin. Clyde laughed at this story and said it was all just foolishness. There's no such thing as a ghost. When you're dead, you're dead was Clyde's refrain. The stories continued.

Being an enterprising young man, and perhaps, a little high in his hooch, Clyde saw an opportunity to make a little money as this group of men was inclined to wager on anything. He held his stick up in the air and declared he "wasn't scared of no ghosts," and issued a challenge. If anyone would give him $0.50, he would take the stick he had been whittling and drive it into Buster's grave to prove he was dead and "weren't no ghost." After some discussion and a collection of coins to equal $0.50, the men called his bluff, certain he would back out. Clyde arrogantly took the dare and stood his ground, knowing he would be $0.50 richer before the evening was finished.

The men gathered hats and coats and walked toward the church and cemetery. The sky was now pitch black and beginning to mist rain, but they were brave walking in a group. Clyde led arrogantly swinging his stick and singing some ditty about no such things as ghosts. They found their way to Buster's grave. Trepidation crept in and one of the men insisted that they say a prayer before commencing this exercise. Another said he thought it might be a good idea to sing a hymn so as not be blasphemous. Then it was time for Clyde to do the deed.

The men formed a circle around the fresh plot of dirt where Buster was buried earlier in the day. Their mood turned somber after the praying and singing. Several expressed doubts about the activity and were ready to head home. Clyde became adamant that he was going to bury the stick in Buster's grave and claim his $0.50.

Clyde moved toward Buster's grave. He knew the stick would have to approach the area of Buster's heart to be good showmanship for his friends. He placed his feet in the loose dirt and rocks on each side of the grave so that he was low to the ground straddling the site. With much fanfare and stretching of arms, he bent over, and placed his sharpened stick right in the middle of the grave. He pulled a clawhammer from his coat pocket, aligned his stick, and proceeded to pound it into the grave with much bravado.

When the stick was about two feet into the dirt, Clyde tried to straighten up. He stopped midway because he felt something pulling on him; something had a hold on him and the more he pulled the tighter the hold. Clyde got scared, dropped the hammer, and started hollering that Buster's ghost was pulling him into his grave. He tried to run, but all he did was throw up clods of dirt and rock. He fell on his face. The stick abruptly came out of the dirt and hit him on backside. Chaos ensued as a parade of men ran blindly through the graveyard causing quite a commotion as they tripped and fell over tombstones yelling about ghosts.

It was the next day before Clyde saw the tell-tale rip in his raincoat. In the dark the night before, he didn't realize he nailed his stick into the grave through the tail of his long raincoat. He was too embarrassed to confess that Buster's ghost was simply his own mistake and fear overtaking him. Buster's ghost and Clyde's lost money were relegated to tales told at gatherings for many years.

FOOTBALL UNDER THE LIGHTS

The old adage, necessity is the mother of invention, is true; however, it may also be said that necessity can serve as an agent for entrepreneurship. The latter was the case in Huntsville, Alabama during the football season of 1934, when necessity propelled two distinctly different entrepreneurs, a men's club and a child, to memorable action at the new Goldsmith-Schiffman Memorial Athletic Field.

By 1934, football fever was rampant in Huntsville, and schools, public service groups, individuals, and government entities were actively engaged in improving gridiron opportunities for young men. The latest effort was the Goldsmith-Schiffman Memorial Athletic Field. On January 25, 1934, the Goldsmith-Schiffman family generously donated the Beirne Avenue property to the city of Huntsville to construct a new football field.

Construction of the new athletic field began almost immediately under the Civil Works Act of Franklin Roosevelt's New Deal Recovery Effort in the winter of 1933. Although the Act was short-lived, it created employment and economic relief for Depression weary citizens, while providing monies to local authorities to fund public projects. For the Goldsmith-Schiffman Project, the Civil Works Act provided $6,500.00 in labor and materials.

Goldsmith-Schiffman Memorial Field was constructed in

approximately nine months. Large chunks of native stone held together with thick gray mortar were used to construct the eight-foot-high perimeter fence of the field. The main entrances featured turret-like columns topped with blunted concrete spires. Ticket selling gates had openings shaped similarly to the turrets with small enclosed booths constructed of the same stone. Bleachers were built on both the north and south sides of the field with a concession area at the west end. A wooden press booth was located atop the bleachers on the south side of the field.

As the field neared completion in the late summer of 1934, local leaders and school officials began to play with the very progressive idea of lighting the field for night games. Those in charge speculated that football games under electric lights would encourage greater attendance and result in higher gate receipts. Increased gate receipts were required to retire the enormous $1.000.00 debt already incurred to equip and outfit the Crimsons in their new, bright red jerseys.

Lighting the field was no small task. Expensive equipment, including the poles, connections, and 32 immense arc bulbs with 48,000-watt light were needed to illuminate the field. The City School Board agreed to the lighting if an entrepreneur to finance this project could be found. The Acme Club, a young men's organization designed to promote the moral, social, and commercial welfare of the city stepped up to the challenge and agreed to underwrite the cost of the project; thus, becoming the first entrepreneur of this story.

To fund the lighting of the field, the Acme Club, with the help of the Huntsville Times, printed 500 season tickets to sell to the community. Club members guaranteed sales of at least 300 season tickets each at $2.50 per ticket to cover the initial down payment on the lighting. And, as most good entrepreneurs do, the Acme Club enlisted help from the Kiwanis, Rotary, and Civitan Clubs. It was a worthwhile cause and enjoyed strong community support.

The first game played at the new Goldsmith-Schiffman Memorial Field was between Huntsville and Limestone County

High Schools, two well-matched teams who enjoyed a good rivalry. The game was played at 3:15 on Friday afternoon, September 27, 1934, to an impressive crowd of approximately 750 fans. Numerous children watched free perched atop the rock walls until the adults removed them. Huntsville High School had a strong starting lineup. Both teams had forward walls and backfields averaging 160 pounds. The Crimsons made a good showing, scoring in every quarter except the fourth. Long, spectacular runs brought the crowd to their feet, roaring approval. A clean game and a good win, 45 to 0, was a positive omen for the following week's game which would also be dedication day for the new field.

The second entrepreneur in this story makes his timely appearance just outside the perimeter of the field prior to the second game. It seems a young, Black boy about 10 years of age, was not only a football fan, but quite an enterprising fellow. He had watched the first game of the season from a secure vantage point provided by a fork in an old oak tree adjacent to the northeast corner of the rock-walled field. His viewing site may have been necessary because of his race and the Southern culture of the day, or it may have been financially rooted as this was during the Depression. Either way, this clever little boy saw the situation in an opportunistic manner. Before the dedication game, he cleaned out his dad's scrap lumber pile, and created seats running from the bottom to the top of that old oak tree, along with rungs for climbing. He had cheap seats that were just little planks nailed to tree limbs, and he had grandstand seats that consisted of two planks forming a seat and a back on upper limbs. Cheap seats costed a nickel and grandstand seats costed a dime.

October 5, 1934, Huntsville High and Gadsden High met at a well-lit Goldsmith-Schiffman Memorial Field in the pouring rain. This fierce rivalry had, for the past four years, resulted in Gadsden victories, but everyone was certain that the Crimsons would win. By 8:00 p.m., a noisy parade of vehicles decorated with soggy red, white, and blue crepe paper arrived at the field. The motorcycle officer that led the group was gone, seeking drier ground. The young Black boy had "hawked" both his cheap and grandstand seats, and hundreds of fans had entered the field. The coin was tossed and the game began. Despite a miserable, cold rain that fell the entire evening, approximately 1,000 fans viewed the game with another 30 in the tree bleachers outside. Some observers noted that the young entrepreneur's patrons had the best seats at the field, not only because they could see so well, but also because the old oak tree had not shed its leaves, thus providing some shelter from the rain. Fans inside and out braved the elements to watch Huntsville beat Gadsden, 19-6, in the first nighttime football game ever played in Huntsville.

During the halftime intermission, a member of the City School Board stood proudly in the glaring light and pouring rain and accepted the field for the school and expressed appreciation to the Huntsville citizens who donated the property. Citizens of Huntsville were thanked for their role in lighting the field and establishing a new era in Huntsville football.

Six more games were scheduled for the 1934 season, all of which were played under the lights with record attendance and gate receipts, both for the school and the young boy. Thunderous cheers sounded and pompoms waved exuberantly with each promising play. And, sometimes, especially with touchdowns, the cheers were accompanied by a gentle shower of colorful oak leaves raining down on the field adding to the revelry of the night, and the absolute wonder of watching a football game played under the lights.

BAD BEGINNING, GOOD ENDING

It was cold and sleeting on the day of December 23, 1938 when the young man arrived at his girlfriend's house. He parked the Model A down by the barn where it was hidden. With his coat collar turned up against the wind, he walked the short distance to the house. The concrete steps were glazed with ice and treacherous, so he climbed very carefully. He was nervous as he surveyed the windows for light. Was anyone awake? The wooden planks of the porch right in front of the door creaked as he tiptoed near. Just as he reached the front door, it opened to him tentatively. The young lady on the other side of the door was obviously waiting for him. He took her suitcase and her arm as she closed the door. They walked down the steps, and into the borrowed car. The young couple quietly left. They went to Huntsville to a Justice of the Peace where they were married. From there they went to his family's home for their honeymoon.

The next morning the girl's parents discovered a note telling of her elopement with her young man. He was a handsome young man, but he was not what her parents wanted. She was only nineteen years old and still in college. Dating and marriage were to be postponed until much later. After all, the girl's mother was twenty-five and her dad was thirty-five when they married. Not only was their daughter marrying too young, but the young man was not one they would have chosen. He was uneducated

the fun we had together. When a faint smile would cross her face, or she would open her eyes, Dad would sweep the gray wisps of hair off of her face just as lovingly as if she were his own mother. I remember somewhere in those long nights that he thanked her again for not returning her first Christmas gift from him. Suddenly, Dad's eyes shot over to me to ascertain whether I recognized what he had said. I pretended to be engrossed in the magazine in front of me. I didn't want Dad to know that I knew that Grandma and Grandad did not want him to marry their daughter. Ironically, it was December 23rd when Grandma died, forty-one years to the day that my Dad entered her life. She gently slipped away from us in the night to join her husband in her new home in heaven, just as her daughter and her young man slipped away from her so many years ago to find a new life.

Life has a funny way of resurrecting things, providing a postscript. I wrote this story almost 20 years ago. At that point my parents and grandparents were all gone. The writing helped me deal with the collective void I was feeling. Then, one day quite out of the blue, a cousin called me asking for my current address. She had something she knew I would want. It was an item found wedged between the wooden mantle and the wall of the homeplace, hidden for so many years. A few days later, a yellowed letter arrived dated December 27, 1938, and addressed to my grandparents from my mother and dad. The letter contained, in my mother's beautiful penmanship, a poignant apology for marrying without their permission, but also a declaration of the young couple's love for each other and their decision. In the letter she assured her parents and brothers of her love. Just three days after their elopement, with this letter, they began work to change what others saw as a bad beginning and make it a good ending. And, by all accounts, it was an excellent ending.

The Homeplace

Drawing by Xienna Khim

HOME FOR THE HOLIDAYS

During the Christmas season the television is full of touching commercials. One of my favorites is a coffee commercial where the young soldier comes home unexpectedly and surprises the family. The desire for a family to be together during the holidays is universal and reminds me of one of the greatest gifts my grandparents ever received. It was a gift that money couldn't buy.

The summer of 1942 should have been a time of unbridled celebration for my grandparents and their children living in Hurricane Valley. Both sons' educational achievements were cause for rejoicing. The younger son finished his first semester in college on a basketball scholarship, and the elder son finished his freshman year of college. The boys would spend most of the summer at home helping bring in what looked to be a bumper crop. Their daughter, my mother, was in college also, and had given them their first precious grandson. All in all, the family was content, but that contentment was fleeting. A terrible war raged overseas, and both boys volunteered for service that summer. A pall descended on the family that lasted three hard years.

Basic training for the younger son began on December 8, 1942, with advanced training as a Heavy Mortar Crewman following. After shipping out on the Queen Mary, he fought the next three years in southern France, Rhineland, Naples Foggia,

Rome Arno, and the Central Europe Campaigns. He was captured by the Germans and held as a prisoner for two weeks. Late one evening as the Germans were marching the prisoners down a dirt road to a holding area, a single U.S. plane strafed the group. He and the man to whom he was shackled escaped during the melee to a broken culvert overgrown with tall weeds. They crawled in the muddy culvert, pulled the broken concrete pieces over them, straightened the weeds, and remained there until the Germans rounded the prisoners up and left. Once they found an Allied group they rejoined the fighting. He was scheduled for invasion training of Japan, but after five campaigns, soldiers were discharged. With no notification, he began the long, welcome journey home.

The elder son joined the U.S. Army on July 22, 1942. His specialty was a computer fire director and a marksman with an M1 carbine. His job was to calculate the trajectory of the Army's big guns using horizontal, vertical, and distance data to insure strikes. He served in northern France and Rhineland Campaigns. While in France, a German Panzer tank fired a 20mm shell into the bunker where five men were doing reconnaissance on November 14, 1944. Four members of the team were killed. He survived but was severely wounded. Shrapnel wounds to his hands, legs, and back gave him his ticket home. He was shipped to an Augusta, Georgia veterans' hospital where he recuperated for almost two years. He never fully regained use of his appendages.

After three hard Christmases, 1945 did not look any more promising for the family. The elder son was still in the hospital in Georgia, but he would recover. My grandparents traveled there to see him and brought him a homemade fruit cake to cheer him. The younger son was still engaged in active fighting in Europe and they had not received a recent Vmail from him which accelerated their worry. Their daughter, her husband, and grandson would spend Christmas with them.

Without any prior notification, the younger son was literally pulled out of invasion training for Japan and shipped out of Naples, Italy to Newport News, Virginia where his discharge was completed on December 23, 1945. From there he traveled by train to Atlanta and caught a Greyhound bus to Huntsville, Alabama. He arrived about 3:00 a.m. No telephone service existed where his parents lived, so no way to call. Taxis did not run that far out in the country, especially at three in the morning. As he sat there at the bus station, he wondered how he would get home. He thought about walking, but it was a very long way and spitting snow. An old man approached and commented on his uniform. They started talking. He had served in WWI and knew of the boy's parents. The man understood the dilemma faced by the young soldier and volunteered to drive him home.

The sun was just coming up when the younger son knocked on his parents' door that Christmas Eve. Grandma answered. She was astonished that he was home, healthy, and discharged from service. She ran to wake Grandad. Coffee was made, just like in the popular commercial, and the three of them talked and expressed prayers of thanksgiving.

The nightmare that was WWII was over for this family, but not without residual effects. I can't even begin to imagine the relief and joy they felt at having both sons stateside and out of the war. It would be some time yet before the elder son returned home from the rehabilitation hospital. But on Christmas Eve 1945, my grandparents were blessed that their loved ones were all on home soil and survived the great war. Not everyone in Hurricane Valley would be so fortunate.

LIFE'S LESSONS AND A BUTTER CHURN

As a little girl growing up in the country in the 1940s, I observed and internalized daily life on my grandparents' farm. Even before I was old enough to understand the quality of their character or work ethic, I somehow knew these people were special. I had an appreciation for them that defied words then and still does today.

The most mundane, daily activities of farm life seemed to take on a spiritual nature with my grandparents, not unlike Sunday worship. For example, the routines associated with bringing milk and butter to our table were not just habit or work, but were reverential toward God and appreciative of all His glorious nature.

Before dawn every morning my grandparents began a long, hard day's work. Grandad started the fire in the old, wood burning iron stove while Grandma trekked out to the smokehouse and cut off a slab of bacon or ham and cooked it with eggs, grits, apples, coffee, and piping hot biscuits served with homemade butter and some of last summer's jams. While preparing breakfast, Grandma, the daughter of a circuit riding preacher, sang hymns while cooking.

After firing up the cookstove, Grandad drew from the well two buckets of fresh water for the kitchen and two buckets for himself. Then he headed to the barn with me following behind.

As he walked through the open, center section of the barn whistling and clanging his metal buckets together, he stopped and grabbed several ears of dry corn from the corn crib and stuffed them in pockets, either in overalls or a flannel jacket. He greeted all the animals by name and they greeted him in return. The mules, chickens, cows, and cats each responded in their own way, and as he worked his way through the barn a parade of uncorralled animals followed. When he reached the shed where the milk cows were housed he stopped and called each by name and petted them. He usually named the milk cows after the young kids in the area. His favorite cow of all time, Mary Jo, was a prolific milk producer. He gave each cow an ear of corn. Still talking to them, he pulled down his three-legged stool, placed his pail full of water under the cow's udder and positioned himself to milk. First, he washed the cow's teats and udder and apologized for the coldness of the water. He always asked her if she had been in the pasture bitterweed or if she had found any new patches of clover. With a good-natured laugh, he set up a rhythm by pulling two teats in turn, delivering quick spurts of milk into his clean buckets. The cats he kept for rodent control positioned themselves around the cow he was milking. Grandad would squirt a stream of warm milk toward each cat's mouth. The accuracy of Grandad's aim and the ability of the cats to catch those streams of milk amazed me. After he finished milking the first cow, he would thank her and move on to the next. This process was repeated until he milked all three of his cows. Following milking, the cows were turned out to pasture with a goodbye pat on the rump. After milking, numerous cats could always be seen lying in the sun outside the cow shed grooming themselves.

Buckets of fresh, warm milk were taken to the house to be processed after breakfast. The milk was strained to remove any straw or grass that might have blown into the buckets during milking. On cold mornings, the warm milk was used immediately on oatmeal or in coffee. The remaining milk was poured into clean quart jars with lids and then carefully lowered inside a long, cylindrical metal pipe into the old sulphur well outside the back door to be used for drinking and cooking. The sulphur well water was not good to drink due to smell and taste, but the depth of the well and the cold water kept the milk fresh.

Fresh, sweet unpasteurized milk deemed for butter and buttermilk was poured into a churn that had been sterilized with boiling water. Then the milk was allowed to clabber or ripen. Clabbered milk, similar to yogurt, was sometimes served for breakfast with spices, honey, or molasses, or used as leavening agent for baking. In the churn, the cream rises and the milk becomes slightly thicker with globules of fat as a result of time, warmth, and beneficial bacteria. In the summer, milk clabbered in two to three hours, but in the winter the containers of milk were placed behind the iron stove and turned several times during the day until this physical process was complete. Grandma would check the milk regularly to see if it had clabbered sufficiently. She would tilt the container to see if the milk held together and pulled away from the sides, and if a certain pungent odor was present. From watching her, I decided it was a fine art to determine the correct degree of clabber. Churning too soon resulted in sour milk that would not make good, sweet butter, and leaving the milk too long resulted in separation which also compromised the quality of the butter.

When the milk was sufficiently clabbered, Grandma started the process using a churn that was a five-gallon tan colored, cylindrical shaped stoneware jar with a lid that had a hole in the middle to hold the wooden dasher. I remember it also had some blue writing on the side. With the churn half full of clabbered milk, Grandma would arrange herself in a special, straight back chair that was very low to the ground and began to test the setting. She moved the chair and the churn next to the screened back door in the summer or near the iron stove in the winter, not only for comfort, but to insure the best temperature for making butter. As soon as she was satisfied that the temperature and drafts were acceptable, she inserted the dasher in the churn. The dasher looked like an X with a long, broom handle attached which fit into the stoneware lid. The dasher was then moved up and down in a rhythmical fashion going all the way from the top to the bottom of the churn violently agitating the milk to separate fat from liquid. Once she established the rhythm and heard the sound she wanted, she turned the churning over to me along with a book.

I churned with my right hand, as I read orally and turn the pages with my left hand. It was while I was churning I discovered the wonder of books. I read Grandma's choices such as *Rose Red, Snow White, Gulliver's Travels*, and *Alice in Wonderland* over and over. My reading/churning went on for 30-45 minutes, and both the reading and churning were expected to maintain a certain pace. Grandma was quick to intervene if either sound was "off."

Grandma would periodically check the contents of the churn. When she deemed the process done she would gather the clumps of fat together from the top of the milk with a flat, wooden paddle. She then poured the remaining buttermilk slowly through cheesecloth to gather more of the globules. All the clumps of butter were placed in cheesecloth over a bowl to drain. Fresh, cool water was poured slowly over the butter to freshen it and lessen spoilage, and it was drained again. The mound of butter was placed on a wooden board and worked with the paddle to remove more liquid and smooth the texture. A little salt was added, and the light-colored butter was packed down into a circular, glass butter mold. Once molded the butter would be patted again and again to remove excess liquid. Grandma was very quick in turning the mold in circles with her left hand and using the wooden paddle with her right hand to press out the liquid. She kept her butter molds in the sulphur well so they would be cold and the butter easier to mold. The final touch was her decorative indentions. She always used the same pattern, two indentations, equal marks, at north, south, east, and west. The butter was then covered with cloth and lowered into the sulphur well on top of the milk already stored there. Buttermilk was jarred and stored in the well also.

I learned to read and to love reading churning butter. We

didn't have a great many books, but each one was a treasure to be savored again and again. My grandma always gave me a new book for Christmas, and she wrote little stories about her life in the Territory of Oklahoma for me to read while I churned. She was always there shelling peas, snapping beans, peeling potatoes, making jams, or doing something constructive while I churned. I believe that in the process of milking cows and churning butter, I learned profound lessons about life including a love of reading, compassion towards animals, a strong work ethic, respect for nature, and an understanding and appreciation of how meaningful life's daily chores are when accompanied by a spiritual attitude as demonstrated by my grandparents.

OUTHOUSE HUMOR

Every person from a certain time period probably has an outhouse story. The setting and its purpose lends itself to unlimited humor. The outhouse itself was an experience. It was usually made out of wood and could be a one, two, or three holer. Somehow, I never think of the outhouse as a social opportunity, but apparently many people did. Chamber pots were used mainly by ladies or for nighttime urges. These were emptied in the outhouse in the morning.

Outhouse construction was either a pit or a bucket design. The pit was a hole in the ground about four feet deep with a round seat cut out from what we might call a shelf directly above the hole. A good depth was required to prohibit splash-back. What went in that hole stayed in that hole until another outhouse was dug and the first one filled in with dirt. The other, less common outhouse, was the bucket type. This type had, as it sounds, a bucket which was emptied as needed. Some cities even had sanitation workers that would empty your bucket on a set schedule. The seat was designed the same way as a pit outhouse. Flush mechanisms were not featured in outhouses as no running water, sewers, or septic tanks were available.

The structure housing the outhouse was usually a small, simple wood house with a roof vent for ventilation. Sometimes it had small windows. The door often featured a moon or a star which dictated female or male respectively. Construction ranged from simple to quite ornate. Some were even brick, hence, the phrase, ". . . built like a brick outhouse." They were usually located away from the main house to inhibit odor and flies. Catalogues were used for toilet paper and lime was sprinkled in the hole upon completion of business to aid with decay and odor. Some people burned the used catalogue pages rather than fill the hole with unnecessary waste. Aside from the obvious difficulties with the outhouse, it was often the site of unusual happenings. That's where the entertainment side of the outhouse appears.

Grandad built their outhouse a good distance away from the house. It was a one holer, and the Sears catalogue was there for cleaning and reading. I also remember dried corn cobs for cleaning purposes. Not easy on the bum! The outhouse was on an incline with a path cut between two rows of trees. The incline was to ensure that liquid from the outhouse did not infiltrate groundwater wells. It stood very close to the mountains, so animal infiltration was a problem. One time, late at night, Grandad went to the outhouse. He did not carry a lantern with him because the moon was full, and in the dark outhouse he did not see that it was already occupied. A mother skunk with her babies found a warm spot for the night and didn't appreciate the loss of privacy. Grandad, half asleep, hit a baby skunk with his foot as he was sitting down and it made a noise. Mama skunk was on the shelf with the cutout seat. Grandad lifted his white, flowing night shirt and mama skunk took that as a threat. She started growling, spitting, fluffing her fur, shaking her tail, and stamping her feet. Then she lifted her tail and sprayed musk directly on Grandad before he could get up from the seat. Stumbling around with his eyes and nose burning, he stepped on another skunk who hit him with a second dose of musk. These nocturnal skunks retaliated for being disturbed. Grandma became aware of the situation, not because of the noise, but the smell. She met Grandad outside of the house with jars of tomato juice. She made him ditch his clothes outside and bury them in the garden. She doused him with the tomato juice and he bathed in the cold water of the animal watering trough, but the odor was still too strong. Grandad slept in the hayloft in the barn that night. He was asked later if he killed those skunks. Grandad just laughed and stated that he would never kill a skunk as they help keep snakes under control. Odor is a small price to pay for snake control.

Mom and Dad built their house in Huntsville before water and sewer utilities were available, so they had an outhouse too. It was just a simple structure that Dad made from tree trunks he harvested from my grandparents' farm. It was to be a temporary structure as the city promised utilities would be available soon. Times were hard and utilities were slow to come to their area, so the outhouse was in use longer than expected. One day Mom was sick and home alone. She found herself in the outhouse frequently that day. As she sat there, her new neighbor pulled up in a strange car. This neighbor was "high falutin," regarding her three-room house. She tended to be negative and easy to anger. As Mom was sitting in the outhouse, her neighbor got out of this unfamiliar car with an unfamiliar man. Mom saw what was happening through gaps between logs of the outhouse. The man seemed to be intimate with the neighbor, kissing her. Mom did not think he was her brother. This intimacy went on for quite a while.

Mom faced a dilemma. If she left the outhouse, then the neighbor would know that she had seen this questionable behavior and she might fear Mom would tell her husband. If she remained cloistered in the outhouse she had no idea how long she might be there. It was a choice between her discomfort and the possibility of destroying a neighborly relationship that had just begun. Mom stayed in the outhouse and she and the neighbor became friends. That friendship lasted many, many years, and she never told the story of the outhouse while that neighbor lived.

Outhouses were often a challenge for kids. First, unless special adaptations were made, the holes were too big for little kids. Most people with little kids who were trained put planks across the seat to ensure that they did not fall in. Kids are curious. They often liked to look in the hole and see what was there. The story is told of two little boys who wanted to fish Pin Hook Creek and decided they could find nice worms for fishing in the outhouse. It was not a bad idea in that worms and insects did live in the outhouse wastes. One boy later said that he had seen the biggest worm ever in the bottom of the pit of the outhouse. He climbed on the seat and with a hoe tried to capture worms. He became unbalanced and fell in the hole. The hole was slick, and no rough spots could he find to pull himself out. His friend decided to help him by pulling him out, but he fell in too. They yelled for help, but like most outhouses they were a distance from any habitation. Mom did not start hunting the boys until dinner time because they had told her they were going fishing. After exhausting all the usual places these boys went, they checked the outhouse. There they were sitting in stinky wastes up to their chests. Dad reached in and pulled each one out while Mom readied a tub of water for washing. Both boys were cleaned of the wastes and lime and vowed to never dig for worms in the outhouse again. Mom stated that she could still smell the boys a week later.

Today's sparkling clean and decorated bathrooms are a long way from the old outhouse. Toilet paper has become a profitable product, along with disinfectants and freshening sprays. It makes one question, at least for a moment, if that old manner of dealing with human wastes might be better for our immune system and infection fighting. Do we have too much cleanliness now? No way, not even if my immune system suffers, would I ever want to go back to the old system. The good old days weren't always so good, especially the outhouse!

WHERE'S THE PORK?

Well, I can tell you in the 1940s it wasn't in the grocery store for my family.

It was in my grandparents' smokehouse hanging from rafters over a smoking fire or stacked on shelves covered in salt. It was good. Today a trip to the grocery store boggles the mind with the variety of food that is available with no more work than taking the item off the shelf or out of the cooler and putting it in the basket. It easy to forget that things were not always so simple. As a young child, I saw and learned to appreciate the work required to insure a family's food supply. Instead of the neighborhood grocery store, it was gardens, milk cows, chickens, orchards, hogs, and expenditures of time and energy that are difficult to imagine in today's world. Procuring the year's pork supply was just one those expenditures.

Each year as the weather turned cool, thoughts turned to hog killing. Hogs that had roamed free on the fenced mountain land were rounded up and placed in a smaller fenced area to fatten. The hills provided plenty of food such as acorns, chestnuts, and persimmons, but to sweeten the meat, hogs identified for killing were fed corn, buttermilk, and table slop for about a month prior to killing. Usually around the middle of December, when daytime temperatures hovered in the 30s, Grandad would announce hog killing time, a season to kill and cure the pork that would provide food for the coming year.

Before we actually began hog killing, many preparations had to be made. Two hard, hickory "end" poles with forked tops were cut and driven deep into the ground about four feet apart in the hog killing area. A new "stout" pole was set in the forks of the "end" poles to make a Y. This contraption would hold even the heaviest hog upright. Also, a large, iron wash pot was set into place with ample firewood underneath and beside it to keep water boiling hot for sterilization and lard rendering. The saltbox in the smokehouse was also filled.

Hogs had to be killed, bled, and cleaned first. Targeted animals, usually three female hogs weighing between 200-250 pounds, were roped around the neck and brought to the killing area one at a time. Then a man hit the hog in the head with a single, double bitted axe to kill her quickly. Then the hog was stuck with a large knife near the jugular vein on the left side of the neck. When the hog bled out she was dragged over to the wash pot for scalding. Grandad and his hired help dipped the animal in hot water to loosen the spiny, little hairs. The skin was scraped, and the process repeated again and again until most of the hog hair was removed from the hide.

Next, the hamstrings on the hind legs were exposed and a sharpened stick was used to make an opening in the tendons on both legs. The "stout" pole was slipped through the open tendons in the hog's legs and then the animal and the pole were hoisted up onto the forked supports. With the hog's head hanging down, the animal was again scalded and scraped until Grandad deemed her clean.

The next step in the process was to cut off the hog's head. A cut was made at the base of the neck separating the head from the backbone. The head was then twisted off. The carcass was allowed to drain. After draining, a long cut was made on the underside of the animal from one end to the other to reveal the entrails. Grandad always made that cut himself because great care was needed not to nick or rupture the membrane around the intestines since that would sully the meat. Grandad would separate and tie off the intestines at the beginning and end of the tract. This would free the entrails from the hog's body. With that accomplished, he would slice open the membrane that covered the intestines and allow them to fall into a #2 washtub under the animal. Grandad then rewashed the inside and outside of the hog with scalding water. Internal organs like the liver, heart, lungs, and stomach were cut free and put in water to soak. The animal was allowed to drain once more, and then removed to a cutting area made up of saw horses and wooden boards that had been scrubbed clean and sterilized.

Cutting began with Grandad using a sharp axe to chop down both sides of the hog's backbone. Then, the prized tenderloin, next to the backbone, was removed and soaked. Removal of the fatback, rib cage, shoulders, and hams came next. The ribs were cut into sections for canning. The hams, shoulders, and middlin' meat were cut into useable sizes and taken to the smoke house as quickly as possible where they were rolled and rolled in salt. Grandad used to say in a sing-song voice, "Don't let the carcass get cold, get the salt, stop the mold." He always left his meat in salt for six weeks as that insured the necessary degree of salt penetration was accomplished regardless of the thickness of the cut. It usually took about ten pounds of salt for every hundred pounds of meat. The salt cured the meat by pulling out excess moisture and animal taint.

Grandad had a closed smokehouse, one with very little space between the slats forming the walls. This design kept out insects and animals. Shelves at different heights were found all around the walls. As you entered, the wall on the right contained a huge saltbox with a wooden lid. In the middle of the smokehouse was a rectangular smoke pit with a dirt floor and stave poles over it for hanging meat. The smokehouse held the meat during both stages of preservation. First, when the weather was cold enough to keep the meat from spoiling, the salted meat was placed on the shelves with a little distance among the pieces. Ventilation was necessary to keep the meat in good form. When a ham or streak of lean was needed, you simply cut off what you wanted, cleaned, soaked, parboiled, and cooked it. Middlin' meat was called streak of lean at this time. It became bacon when it was smoked in the next step of the preservation process. As temperatures began to warm, about April, the second stage of the preservation process, smoking, began. Meat was taken out of the salt, washed and covered with a preserving mixture. Grandad's preserving mixture was a syrup of black pepper, molasses, brown sugar, and borax. The mixture was applied thickly, and then the meat would be bagged in old flour sacks that were washed and saved from year to year. Bagged meat would then be pierced with oak splints to hang the meat over the fire pit. The fire was built from scalybark chips and dried corn cobs. Thick smoke billowed out of the smoke house for a week or two until the meat turned crusty brown. The brown crust sealed the meat from insects. Early on spring mornings in the mountains, wispy smoke and sweet-smelling odors filled the air from smokin' season.

Sausage making was also part of the hog killing process. Pieces of meat with good lean-to-fat ratios were set aside for grinding. Trimmings from hams, shoulders, middlin' meat and tenderloin were run through a manual meat grinder and mixed with spices to make the sausage. Each cook had her own recipe for sausage, some hot and some mild. Grandma used salt, brown sugar, black pepper, sage, garlic, and red pepper. After grinding, a #2 washtub would be almost full. Then the sausage would be partially cooked, cased, and hung in the smokehouse. Casings were made from clean flour sacks sewn to size. If the sausage was to be flat, a rolling pin was used to achieve desired thickness. Flour sprinkled at the open end of the rectangular sack combined with moisture made a paste that sealed the casing. If the casing was round then strings tied the ends. Sometimes, Grandma used the caul, a membrane covering the intestines, as casings. Sausage went into a specific location in the smokehouse.

Backbones and ribs were usually canned. Ribs were cut into two-inch sections and the backbones were separated at each vertebra. Together these parts were stewed in large, three-legged iron kettles on the stove. Salt and other spices were added.

Grandma made a particularly good set of barbeque spices that she added to the kettle. Then the meat was pressure canned.

Fat rendering was also an important part of the hog killing process. Fat was trimmed from the various cuts of meat and left outside, covered, overnight. In the morning, fat chilled by the cold night air was easier to cut into plum sized pieces. Those pieces of fat were placed in an iron wash pot with just a little water and soda and cooked all day. A wooden "juggin" stick that looked a little like a boat paddle was used to keep the lard moving. It required constant stirring. After cooking all day the fat melted, the water evaporated, and the little crunchy cracklins remained. These cracklins were saved to make cracklin cornbread and for nibbling. After the rendered lard cooled, it was poured into five-gallon, galvanized buckets. The lard was not usually snowy white and solid, but more of a beige color and a semi-liquid consistency. Darker and stronger oil resulted when hogs fed more on acorns and chestnuts. Once rendered, the lard was used for frying, baking, and seasoning.

During hog killing time, most people enjoyed fresh pork. Tenderloin with biscuits and gravy was always served. Even though some people used all parts of the hog, Grandma did not. The skin, tail, intestines, stomach, snout, and brains were given to people in the community that liked these parts, and during hard times, these less desirable parts were well received.

Hog killing usually took several people at least three days to finish. Each day started before dawn and ended at dusk, but the result was a smokehouse filled to the brim with pork for the family to eat and share with friends and neighbors. It was a very gratifying experience.

Today when I go the grocery store and pick out some chops or bacon or ham, I remember helping my grandparents with hog killing, and I am thankful for that experience. Within that enormous expenditure of time and energy to provide the family with a year's supply of pork, I learned far too many lessons to ever recount, and I do know where the pork comes from.

GRANDMA'S FLOWER GARDEN

I can still see her in my mind's eye, my grandma. She was a tall, thin, straight woman with long gray hair that she kept pulled back in a figure eight at the nape of her neck. She always wore a mid-calf length, long sleeved cotton dress with a simple design. The dress was covered in a bib apron, and when outside, a sun bonnet protected her head. Her shoes were plain, black and serviceable with circles cut out of the leather on each side to accommodate bunions. Both shoes rolled to the outside significantly and her cotton hose could not conceal ankles distorted by arthritis. She wore wire rimmed glasses. I remember her hands too. They were leathery and age spotted with fingers like gnarled twigs. Altogether, she might have appeared severe if not for her laughing eyes, quick smile, and sweet disposition.

As a young child, I lived with my grandparents on their farm until I was old enough to start school. Memories of both of them abound, but it was Grandma that made the greater impression on me. And, it was in her flower garden that we bonded and spent many wondrous hours together. As we readied ourselves to garden each day, she would say, "The best place to find God is in a garden. You can dig for Him there." I always thought that was original until I read it in a George Bernard Shaw book in college.

Grandma's garden was on the right side of the house. It

banked up against the gravel road with a rock retaining wall that was adorned in spring with purple thrift cascading over it. It was a very large garden, probably thirty-five feet in length and twenty feet across and fenced with weathered cedar staves and chicken wire. A gate was on one end.

When Grandma married Grandad, they moved from Oklahoma to Alabama. The life she left behind was a true prairie life, having even lived in a dugout at one time as part of the Oklahoma Territory saga. She was a school teacher. Her Oklahoma home was special and she became nostalgic talking about the wind driven soil, lack of trees, and the abundant prairie grasses. She lamented that her family never had the resources to develop a flower garden. That, in her words, was a luxury in expenditure of water that was not necessary. The move to Alabama with its plentiful rain and rich soil gave her an opportunity to explore gardening in a way she had never known.

When the young couple moved to their new farm, Grandad, as promised, cleared, fenced, and amended the soil in the area next to the wood frame house for her garden. He also dug channels from the mountain to direct rain water onto the garden, and resurrected an old, undrinkable sulphur well to provide irrigation if needed. It was a barren patch of ground in the 1920s, and with little money to spend on frivolous things, Grandma had to improvise. She walked the woods behind the house hunting plants she could transfer to her garden. Natives such as the pitcher plant, Cahaba lily, wild roses, honeysuckle, passion flower, and yellow eyed grass were all tried. Word also got around in the community that she wanted cuttings. Neighbors, church members, friends, and strangers shared roots and stems and seeds from their supply. Grandma planted, and her garden grew.

During the Depression, many men traveled the route from Tennessee south by way of the farm. These men would often stop and ask about work or food. Grandma always fed them something. Word got out that a meal was available there, and the men would show up with plant rootstock or cuttings in their pockets to repay her kindness.

By the time I journeyed into her flower garden, it was lush and filled to the brim with a riot of color and vast variety. The perimeter of the garden had beautiful shrubs and each one had a story, and as we worked Grandma shared those stories. One of the first plant stories I remember was about a giant snowball bush. It seems an old, Black man brought a young snowball bush to Grandma after she gave the family an old rope bed and some meat from the smokehouse when their house caught fire. It was always a spectacular bush, probably ten feet tall and covered in blooms each spring and beautiful fall foliage. He also brought her some St. Peter's wreath shrubs. I always found a way to make secret rooms out of those graceful, sloping branches.

At some point, a man working on the TVA flood and electricity project traveled by the farm on a regular basis. He would take a meal with my grandparents and share news. He passed through the mountains north of the farm and brought rhododendron roots for Grandma which she planted around the perimeter of the garden. I loved those because they smelled like grapes and had beautiful clusters of purple flowers.

Grandma told me of one young man who would bring clumps of October flowers that looked like asters for the right to hunt squirrels and rabbits on the mountain land every fall. October flowers were found throughout the garden.

Roses were a specialty of my grandma. She had big, old roses that smelled sweet. She propagated them from cuttings people brought her. Red and white ones climbed the garden fence. These special roses were used for Mother's and Father's Days at church. If your parent was living, you wore a red rose, and if your parent was deceased, you wore a white rose. In one corner of the garden was a very special rose. A cutting of it came from a neighbor whose son brought it from England after World War I. That cutting spread throughout the community and most everyone had this miniature pink rose that bloomed so profusely.

As finances improved, seeds were purchased from catalogues. I remember Grandma and I searching these catalogues during the winter months for seeds to plant in the spring. Part of searching the catalogues included translating the listed names of the flowers to names which were familiar to us. Gillyflower was listed as stock or Virginia Flower in the catalogues. Bachelor Buttons were listed as cornflowers, and Granny's Bonnet was called columbine. After ordering the seeds, Grandma would let me cut up the colorful pictures and make play gardens. She had me copy the names of the flowers even though I had not yet started school.

Dahlias, a particularly showy flower in height, color, and size, were Grandma's favorite. She planted a long line of them facing the road where they stood at attention for all to see and admire. Dinner plate sized blooms of all different colors were tied to the fence to prevent the stems from breaking under the weight.

Grandma's garden was a delight not just to our eyes, but one shared with the entire community. Her flowers appeared in church on Sundays, and in her weekly sick calls on neighbors. New babies and their mothers also got a bouquet. These tributes came from her famous cutting garden where annual flowers bloomed from early spring into late fall. Rows of zinnias and daisies were prominent as they made good cut flowers that lasted several days in a vase. I remember walking through rows of daisies where the blooms were at eye level. Larkspur, marigolds, cosmos, candytuft, phlox, and cone flowers accompanied the zinnias in most bouquets.

An herb garden was also part of Grandma's flower garden. Her pantry was filled with drying herbs hanging from the ceiling. Herbs were used in cooking, canning, and for medicinal purposes. Chives, garlic, dill, mint, thyme, rosemary, lavender, and comfrey were just a few that she grew. She often mixed the herbs with honey for medical purposes. She also made poultices with various herbs and flour, water, or bacon grease and applied to the body either hot or cold for congestion, boils, rashes, bruises, arthritis, and to draw out swelling or infection. Grandma made and used herbal teas medicinally. Mint rose hips, and echinacea plants were some of the teas she made to help with insomnia, nervous conditions, and stomach upset. Asphidity bags were smelly concoctions worn around the neck during winter. Composed of a variety of roots, pokeweed, garlic, onion, and ginseng, the bags were used to ward off colds, flu, and pneumonia. I was told the longer it was around your neck, the worse the smell. It was a welcome rite of spring to dispose of the asphidity bag.

Grandma's garden eventually outgrew the space allotted due to her prolific planting and to the plants naturalizing. Then the perimeter of the house was annexed. Hollyhocks, althea bushes, flowering quince, heliotrope, four o'clocks, and lilacs found space there and flourished. Wisteria also found its way onto the hen house and definitely improved the odor. The wisteria climbed, and eventually killed the old cherry tree and several other trees behind the hen house, but it was beautiful.

The front porch received my Grandma's attention next. She built tables by placing planks across the 90 degree corners on both ends of the porch. There she planted petunias that hung down over the railings and smelled wonderful. Also, she planted petunia pots going up and down both sides of the rock steps and platform leading to the house from the dirt road. In front of the house she planted weigela and forsythia. Hummingbirds loved the weigela. I would sit in a rocker on the front porch for hours watching them.

Grandma kept her garden in great condition until her age, 88, compelled her to stop. Even then she would wander out to the front porch overlooking the garden and state that the hollyhocks or the iris were looking especially good this year. Visitors were always invited to pick a bouquet as a parting gesture. The garden was her pride and joy which she generously shared.

The other day I was driving home listening to an oldies station when the words "Where have all the flowers gone? Long time passing," by Peter, Paul, and Mary filled the air. It started me thinking about Grandma and her love of flowers. That love she instilled in me still resonates today as I view my three flats of begonias awaiting planting. Grandma and her beautiful garden are long gone, as is that child of yesterday, but her memory, unlike flowers, will never fade.

POPCORN MAN

In the 1940s, movies were the foremost entertainment in Huntsville. Modern black and white productions with sound such as *Casablanca* with Lauren Bacall and Humphrey Bogart, or *Grapes of Wrath* with Henry Fonda were presented at a trio of theaters including the Lyric, the Grand, and the Elks. And, without a doubt, the most popular snack to accompany the movies was popcorn. The popularity of popcorn fairly exploded during this time period for several reasons. First, popcorn was inexpensive, tasty, and readily available. Second, the taste for the salty treat grew immensely because of the lack of sugar available for sweet treats during World War II. Third, the number of movie-goers increased dramatically with the successful combination of picture and sound, and the post-War emotional and financial climate was conducive to entertainment. Uncle Walt successfully capitalized on the popularity of movies and popcorn, and proudly grew the popcorn that for many years was part of the movie experience in Huntsville.

Uncle Walt, as he was known to everybody, was choosy about his popcorn. His preference was always pearl corn. Pearl popcorn was rounded in shape and smooth, as opposed to rice popcorn which was elongated and bumpier. The pearl corn produced a variety of colors including red, pink, blue, yellow, and multi-colored kernels. Uncle Walt was ahead of his time as he only grew what would be called heirloom popcorn today. This popcorn was open or self-pollinating with the seeds replicating the parent plant. He saved his own harvested seeds to plant next year's crop, and he also bartered with other farmers for unique varieties.

Each spring Uncle Walt planted ten to twelve acres in popcorn. These acres were located on the outside perimeter of his farm so as not to compromise pollination, quantity, or quality of any other crops, particularly sweet corn. The popcorn acreage, just below the mountain land, was also chosen because of the abundance of wet water springs which supplied the corn with plenty of water for optimum kernel development. Tall green corn stalks flourished and bore ears of corn that ripened during the long, hot summer, and came to harvest in the late fall when the entire plant had turned into dry, straw-colored fodder.

For harvesting, two mules were hitched to a wagon and driven through the tall, crackling rows of corn. As the wagon and mules traveled through the field, one or more rows, the "down rows," would be sacrificed for the convenience of using the wagon. Young children were enlisted to help by trailing behind the wagon and picking up those ears that had been knocked down under the wagon. Uncle Walt picked the ears from the standing stalks. Ears of corn covered in dry shucks were pitched into the wagon until the field was harvested.

The overflowing wagon returned to the barn where the ears of corn were hand stripped. The dry shucks were pulled downwards from the top of the ear to form a tail at the end where the corn had been connected to the stalk. Several ears were tied together with a loose shuck and hung-over tier-poles that crisscrossed the corn crib from top to bottom. The harvested ears were left to dry in the cool fall air until he deemed them ready to shell. Ready to shell meant that the corn had moisture content of somewhere between 13% and 17% which determined by shelling sample ears and popping them. If the popcorn was too chewy, then the corn needed to dry more. If the kernels popped up fluffy and tasty, then it was time to shell. Too many "old maids" meant the corn was too dry.

Shelling the popcorn was no easy matter. The corn was very hard and dry and shelling was rough on the hands. A mechanical sheller was not used because of the potential damage to the kernels, *i.e.,* jeopardizing the drop of water at the center of each kernel which, when heated, caused the eruption. And without electricity on the farm, an electric sheller was useless. The popcorn was hand shelled by holding one ear in your left hand and one ear in your right hand and rubbing the two ears together with sufficient force to release the kernels, and hopefully, spare your own knuckles. The little dry kernels rattled as they fell into a small tub, and then that tub was slowly poured into a large #2 washtub from a height that allowed a breeze and gravity to clean any residual chaff or shuck from the kernels. This process was repeated until the corn was clean and free of debris. The cobs were tossed into a pile in the crib for later use primarily as fire-starters.

After the cleaning process, the shelled popcorn was packed into 50-pound burlap sacks which were sewed together with a thick twine. Then he loaded his '45 Chevrolet truck to take the corn to town to fulfill the annual contracts established the previous spring. The contracts were just gentlemen's agreements; handshakes. So, on a fateful fall day about 1948, Uncle Walt set off for town to complete the final task in a nine-month journey of growing and supplying popcorn to all three movie theaters in Huntsville.

In retrospect, Uncle Walt said he should have seen the invasion of Jolly Time Popcorn coming to small town Huntsville infiltrating his market. He had heard about and been entertained by "General Jolly Time and His Popcorn Colonels" on the radio. He had also heard Jolly Time advertised as the "world's best popcorn" by radio personality Arthur Godfrey. This company was so incredibly innovative as to sell popcorn, not in bulk as it had always been done, but in modern, novelty tin cans with snappy logos for .10 each. And, as if to add insult to injury, "a guaranteed to pop" phrase was emblazoned on each can. So, Uncle Walt was not taken totally by surprise when the theaters he contracted with, one by one, told him they had decided to buy their popcorn from Jolly Time. Disappointed, but ever the gentleman, he thanked the managers of the theaters for their long-time business and returned to the truck where a load of unsold popcorn was waiting.

Uncle Walt analyzed the situation and justified the theaters' decisions based on the glitzy cans, ease of storage, price, rodent control, and probable government inspections. But what was he to do with a truck bed full of 50-pound sacks of popcorn? He decided to try to sell it to other commercial dealers in Huntsville. He went to I. Winn Hardware Store first, and there every last kernel of popcorn was purchased. His sizeable investment, his cash crop, was not totally lost, and the hardware store gained a lifelong customer.

Jolly Time, with its progressive marketing strategies and innovative processes, became a world leader in popcorn production. Uncle Walt, the Popcorn Man, never raised popcorn again for public consumption, but the small plot he planted each year kept us supplied with prairie gold, the Native American term for popcorn.

A ROBERT FROST KIND OF DAY

The year my Christmas was defined by scarlet fever was the year that I first met Robert Frost. Oh, not in person, but in his beautiful poetry. During the days when I was confined to bed, quarantined, and bored to tears, Mother began a very special tradition. This tradition is now in its third generation in my family.

It all started with three little plastic deer that I bought in the local five and dime store the week before I got sick. One hazel colored buck with antlers and a white flag for a tail stood tall, head up, sniffing something. The nut-brown doe's head was bending low as if drinking from a cool pond. And the third one, a spotted fawn, was lying down. I played with them all week. They danced across the table by the sofa and accompanied me to the dinner table every night to keep watch. The deer fit perfectly in the pocket of my winter coat, so I took them outside and to school with no one's knowledge. When I got sick, naturally they found their way to my bed where they played in pretend snow drifts made from hills and valleys in the white sheets.

Since Mother was also bedridden due to a sprained ankle, she decided to play my deer games with me. She took the round mirror out of her hand mirror. That became the lake that one deer could drink from. Then she found some cotton batting escaping from an old quilt and made more realistic snow banks. Daddy got in on the game too by bringing in little, brown twigs and green pine needles. He also found an old cardboard box which he covered in white tissue paper to hold the scene. The mirror was glued in the middle and the twigs and greenery placed all around in the white batting. Mom sprinkled Ivory Snow Flakes laundry detergent on the whole scene. Oh, it was beautiful.

Each day we would rearrange the scene. The fawn would hide near the lake or under the pine twigs. As we played, Mom always said the same verses over and over again. I loved the verses and memorized them. The tradition of building the scene continued all through my childhood. Each year we would add a new little animal or two. Sometimes it would be a squirrel or fox or a turtle. The scene was always strategically placed on an end table near the Christmas tree, and the verses repeated numerous times. Winter days with the promise of snow also prompted a repeat of the verses.

I eventually outgrew the scene, and it was packed away in the attic, but the verses never left me. It was a special memory Mother and I shared. One of us would start the verse and the other would finish it. As familiar as the lines were to me, it was not until I was grown and in freshman literature I realized that Mom had taught me Robert Frost's famous poem, "Stopping by the Woods on a Snowy Eve." I marveled at the fact that she never missed an opportunity to teach, and this learning was not only painless, but fun.

The magic of the woodland scene has been experienced by my daughter and her girls. Watching my granddaughters turn away from the TV and gaming to reproduce the scene is always rewarding. Today's snowy woods is created on Styrofoam with many animals, birds, and aerosol snow. The scene serves to stimulate imagination as the children create new stories about the animals daily during the holidays. I have not told them about the author of the verses but am waiting for them to discover Mr. Frost on their own. Although it has been almost 40 years since Mother and I shared this special connection, a Robert Frost kind of day still has the power to stir my memory and bring me to tears.

CHRISTMAS IN A '47 GREEN PLYMOUTH

Huntsville, Alabama in 1950 was like most cities and towns in the United States, very concerned about the international crisis in Korea. President Truman's actions headlined newspapers daily, and strange words such as Chuchon and Pyongyang cropped up in hushed, foreboding adult conversations. However, war talk was generally moderated at the nightly dinner table, and since television and its twenty-four-hour news coverage was not yet a reality, most children remained blissfully oblivious to the turmoil and fear in those days so closely following World War II. I was one of those children steeped in innocence, and fortunate enough to live in a place with a family that sought to maintain the sanctity of childhood regardless of the obstacles.

My family moved back to Huntsville in 1945. Dad worked for Southern Cotton Oil and Mom taught at Rison School. Home was a very unpretentious four room house that my parents built out of concrete blocks on a lot that cost $100.00. The interior walls were made from discarded munitions boxes from World War II. My brother and I always joked that we learned to read and develop some sense of geography by sounding out names such as Malta, London, and Tunisia imprinted on those wooden boxes.

The 1950 Christmas season started off with a great deal of promise, despite world troubles and milk skyrocketing to $0.24 a gallon. Mom and I had been busy preparing gifts, making tin foil tree stars from gum wrappers and baking Grandma's applesauce cake. Then about a week before Christmas, a series of events unfolded that seemed to change our prospects for a great holiday. First, I broke out in a fever and red rash that Mom diagnosed as measles. She put me to bed and darkened the room. In those days, the combination of measles and sunlight was thought to cause permanent eye damage. The second event happened just one day later, Mom fell and sprained her ankle. She joined me in bed, and the doctor was called.

The doctor arrived that very evening. He was such a distinguished looking man, tall with silver hair and penetrating eyes. He began examining Mom's grossly discolored ankle while telling and laughing at his own well-worn jokes. Suddenly, he turned serious and began to examine me more closely. He announced that I did not have measles, but a much more serious disease, scarlet fever, that required quarantine. He instructed Dad to remove my brother from the house and not let anyone come in direct contact with me. This third event certainly did not bode well for a glorious holiday as my brother, grandparents, and extended family would not be able to celebrate with us.

Being a seven-year-old, I began to complain miserably about Christmas being ruined. I was particularly upset about missing the Christmas parade the following Saturday. Mom attempted to allay my distress with games, stories, and songs, and Dad put up a sweet-smelling cedar tree that extended all the way from the corner of the bedroom to the door. Despite their valiant efforts, I would not be consoled, and in an overly dramatic scene, I declared Christmas failed this year.

Early on the afternoon of the Christmas parade, Dad in his old, felt fedora, peeked his head from behind the cedar tree sporting a grin from ear to ear. He told me to get my chin up off the floor as he began stripping quilts off the bed. Still in my pajamas, he tossed me into the middle of the quilts and rolled me up just like I'd seen him roll hundreds of cigarettes. With me giggling and questioning his purpose, he placed me in the back seat of our '47 green Plymouth. After he carried Mom to the car, we drove over to the oil mill which was next to the railroad depot. I could scarcely contain my excitement. I knew we were going to the Christmas parade.

Dad pulled onto the cotton mill property passing mountains of cottonseed hulls all the way back to the rail spur. He worked his way around pull cars, trucks, railroad ties, cotton bales, and other obstacles until we were at the back of the depot where the parade was forming. He knew this was the best spot to see the parade up close.

It was spitting snow and terribly cold even at two in the afternoon. Mom and I snuggled in close together to share our quilts and warmth. I rubbed a ghostly circle on the window, so I could see the parade forming. Chaos reigned with prancing horses, floats, and bicycles with crepe paper streamers wrapped in the spokes and streaming from the handlebars. Children were running everywhere dressed in costumes. Hopalong Cassidy was popular as at least a dozen kids had opted for that costume. One girl wore a blue dress and red shoes like Dorothy from the *Wizard of Oz*, but no coat, despite her mother's efforts. The boy who won the twenty-five-dollar prize was dressed like Daniel Boone, complete with several blue tick hound dogs tied with ropes and all going different directions. A cacophony of sounds filled the air as high school and college bands were doing sound checks and finding their place in the formation.

While we watched the parade forming in the staging area, Dad zipped his coat, turned up his collar, and left the car. A few minutes later he reappeared with Santa in tow. Santa, in his red suit and bigger than life, bent over and peered at me through the frosty window. He didn't say a word, just smiled and waved a white gloved hand at me. I was awestruck and speechless as he walked away and assumed his place at the end of the parade in the Forty *et* Eight Locomotive, a refitted school bus chassis built to resemble a locomotive, decorated to the hilt. Dad later told me that the locomotive honored a group of forty mules and eight heroic men that rode together in a box car in France during World War I. When the Forty *et* Eight Locomotive pulled out, and with the last strains of Christmas music still ringing in my ear, Dad pulled the '47 Plymouth back out onto the street.

After the parade, and a rare take out meal of hamburgers, Dad drove us around town to see the various Nativity scenes at churches. Several had live animals. City buildings also had displays. One spectacular display was a life size replica of Santa's sleigh and eight reindeer high atop the pool house. A living Christmas tree display was set up in front of the courthouse where girls dressed in choir robes stood on a platform in the shape of a tree and sang carols. Dad parked the '47 Plymouth there for a while and rolled a window down just a little to hear the singing until it got too cold. Christmas parade Saturday had turned out pretty good.

I was still sick when Christmas Eve came around, although the quarantine had been lifted and my brother was allowed to come home. Once again the family crawled into the '47 green Plymouth and we drove all around town enjoying the Christmas lights. My brother and I had a contest to see who could count the most Christmas trees shining through the windows of homes. When we got home, Mom made hot chocolate with peppermint candy canes for stirring. We sat on a wooden apple crate in front of the big, old coal stove that Dad stoked up to keep us warm.

Just about the time we sat down, there was a loud commotion outside. Someone was playing "Here Comes Santa Claus" calliope style. Dad flung open the front door and Mom grabbed coats as we joined dozens of other kids from the block. Outside the Forty *et* Eight Locomotive was making a Cracker Jack run down our street. Several of the local citizens clubs teamed up and drove through neighborhoods each Christmas Eve tossing gum, candy, and Cracker Jacks. Santa, doing his big *ho, ho, ho,* was perched on the cowcatcher at the front of the locomotive.

As the locomotive and its flashing lights and sirens left our street, we walked back to the house still picking up candy and gum. I overheard Mom say to Dad somewhat wistfully, "I wonder what Christmas will be like next year. The newspaper said the city merchants are going to increase Christmas activities if this thing in

Korea does not break into a full-scale war." The word war passed through my consciousness in a fleeting fashion, but I was too focused on the really important stuff to questions Mom's comment. After all, it was Christmas Eve and I had been a good girl all year. I was getting well, and all my family would celebrate together. From the corner of my eye, I saw the '47 green Plymouth silhouetted in the night, and somehow I knew that Christmas 1950 had already exceeded my expectations and Christmas morn' was still to come.

COTTON PICKIN' DAYS

I hated cotton pickin'! Let me tell you the reasons I hated picking cotton: It was hot, dirty, hard, and endless.

It was hot. The cotton came in around late summer or early fall when the heat and humidity were at their highest. I wanted to wear shorts and sleeveless shirt for this hot job, but Grandma made me wear long sleeves, long pants, and a big old bonnet to protect my skin, all of which added to my discomfort. Of course, we didn't know about sun exposure and skin cancer then, but I am thankful now that she insisted I wear that old fashioned "get up."

It was dirty. Pulling those big old canvas cotton sacks stirred up a trail of dust behind every picker and it was hard not to eat red dirt all day long. Add to that trail of dust and enough sweat to choke a horse and your skin becomes muddy. Streams of moisture laden dust streak down your face and creep into your eyes. You stop to rub your eyes and your face becomes incredibly dirty. Your fingernails are black all around the cuticles and under the nails. And, even though you are wearing a bonnet, your hair becomes filthy strings.

It was hard. Now, that is an understatement. Pulling that soft, fluffy cotton ball out of each little boll seems innocent enough, but each dried boll has unbelievably sharp points that get you no matter how carefully you twist out the little white part.

You leave the field every day with broken tips of bolls in all kinds of places you didn't even think you touched. Your hands become painfully sore. Hard, because you face endless rows of boring work. The longer you work the longer those rows seem. The strap on the bag cuts a rut in your shoulder that becomes more painful the heavier the sack. The posture needed to pick the cotton means your back is bent too long in the same position and it hurts.

It was endless. My Grandad planted acres of cotton and hired many people to do the picking. The men he hired picked two hundred pounds of cotton a day. I watched them clean a row completely while I still was not half done. Then, when I got called out for goose pickin' the cotton and had to return to areas where I had not picked it clean, that made it seem I would never finish a row. The whole month of September or October or both were spent in cotton picking. That time spent on the cotton rows meant I was not in school, which was where I would have much rather been.

Cotton picking in some form was always part of my life. Even when I was too little to go to the fields, my job was to help feed the workers. Grandma and I would cook mountains of food for the pickers. Cotton picking really whets the appetite. Every day she sliced huge chunks of pork hanging in the smokehouse to boil or fry. She cooked beans, greens, potatoes, corn, and okra to go along with the meat. Her table always included sweet onions, peppers, and pickled beets. Fresh jams, butter, molasses and honey were there for the cornbread which was made in huge rectangular pans. My first job associated with cotton pickin' was to keep the cornbread moving around the tables. Pies, puddings, and cakes were made in abundance and disappeared no matter how many she made. Tea, sweet milk, buttermilk, and cold water were available. And, of course, the work didn't stop after the dinner meal. Dishes had to be cleaned. Some days Grandma would bake bread and send sandwiches to the fields if she had other things to do than prepare a sit-down meal.

As I got older, I took my place in the cotton fields.

Grandma made me a much smaller canvas cotton sack, one that I could actually pull. I would go to the fields right after breakfast along with everyone else, and pick until Grandad would send me to the cotton house where I usually fell asleep. I liked the cotton house because there was always cool water there.

When the pickers filled the wagon with cotton, Grandad would hitch the mules and we would go to the gin. The gin was only about two miles from the house and next to a country store. Grandad usually let me ride with him and gave me a nickel or so to spend at the store while he was waiting his turn in the gin line. He would pull his wagon under this big vacuum like thing and the cotton would disappear. After that we would head home. Grandma would make a simple supper such as milk and cornbread as everyone was tired from the day's work. After a bath in a washtub we went to bed as quickly as possible, usually at sunset, because the next day you would do it all over again. Occasionally the routine was broken by rain, which was not a good thing.

One year the monotony of cotton picking days was broken by an event that will not soon be forgotten. It was near the end of cotton picking season. We still had the Andy piece to pick, which was the smallest of Grandad's fields. It was also a favorite because the ground was level making the sacks easier to drag. That day Grandma brought loads of ham and bread slices, pickles, and cookies to the cotton house. She had a church event that required her attendance, so no sit down meal. When dinner time came around, most of the pickers found respite in the shade of the cotton house sitting on the floor or in the doorway. Grandad opened both doors to the cotton house to allow a draft to cool everyone. We sat there for about 45 minutes, finished our meals, and got ready to knock out the Andy piece. The cotton house was empty except for the pickers having lunch because all the sacks were in use and hoes and shovels had been placed strategically around the field in the morning so that if a snake appeared a weapon would not be too far away.

As Grandad called us back to work after lunch, he picked me up and put me in the wagon and told me to stay there. Then he told some of the men to get their guns. The other pickers started back to work. While the guys were getting their guns, Grandad went to the barn. He came back with bottles of something, maybe kerosene, which he poured around the perimeter of the cotton house. When the men returned, he positioned them surrounding the cotton house. Then he told the rest of the pickers to get in the wagon.

With that done, he set fire to the cotton house. The house was an eight by ten wooden structure with a tin roof. It was old and dry, so the fire was very hot and moved quickly. I stared at him in disbelief. Then I heard gunfire and watched as the men shot things on the ground. The shots were coming quickly. Someone shouted do you hear them thangs a rattlin? I realized that they were killing snakes; rattlesnakes. Goosebumps covered my arms as I was terrified of snakes.

The shooting went on for a while and finally the house was reduced to debris and ashes. Grandad made his way to the cotton house with a hoe in his hands. He used the hoe a couple of times, then called the men to come in. They started hauling dead rattlesnakes out of the ashes and hanging them over the fence. Some were so long they reached the bottom of both sides of the fence. All together about 40 snakes were killed. Grandad raked the coals over and over to make sure no snakes were alive.

That evening Grandad was explaining to Grandma why he burned the cotton house. He said as he was sitting there eating his lunch, he could hear snakes, lots of them. He didn't say anything because he was afraid someone would create a noise or commotion and cause the snakes to come out before he could get everyone to safety. As it was, no one was hurt, and Grandad rebuilt the cotton house. We finished the Andy piece the next day, and gratefully said goodbye to a productive cotton season just in time for the rains to start.

LAWRENCE WELK'S LOST BATON

Mr. Tommie, a wizened old man, had definite tastes in television. His favorite show was the Lawrence Welk Show. He watched it religiously. The show was a 60 minute, highly successful televised musical variety show lead by Lawrence Welk that aired weekly. Originally broadcast in the early 1950s, reruns kept it in public view until many, many years later. The show's format was based on a party-like diversion from life. Mr. Welk, using his baton, would lead the band in a variety of musical selections from waltzes to folk music to polkas. Dancing and singing acts were interspersed between band numbers. Shows revolved around a central theme like the roaring 20s or a Broadway play. Groups such as the Lennon Sisters performed weekly and established a sense of continuity and loyalty with the audience. The shows always ended with Welk inviting the live audience to dance.

After spending so many Saturday evenings watching this show, Mr. Tommie came up with a great idea. He wanted to make a baton on his wood lathe as a gift for Mr. Welk. The wood he wanted to use was shitttam, also called acacia. It is an especially hard wood with a fine grain known to be more durable than oak or hickory. This rare wood was thought to only grew on Monte Sano Mountain in Alabama and in the Sinai Peninsula of Egypt. The Bible mentions this wood in conjunction with Noah, the Arc of the Covenant, and the tabernacle and in numerous verses in Exodus. The biblical connection, strength of the wood, and its potential availability appealed to Mr. Tommie as perfect for constructing a special baton for Mr. Welk.

The story told to me was that a great deal of time was grudgingly spent trying to find the shittam wood on Monte Sano Mountain. Grandsons sought the tree based on the description that it was a fairly slow growing tree, so usually no more than 25 feet tall. Its lifespan was about 30 years. The slow growth and irregular structure, loosely branched and fairly vertical against the main trunk, resulted in a plain silhouette easier to find in winter. The bark was scaly and dark in color. Snap a twig and the interior was orange. Upon finding shittam wood, some of the guys searching expressed doubt as to the use of the wood as mentioned in the Bible because, although it was strong, the tree had a really small trunk no more than 5-6 inches in diameter. This doubt did not reach Mr. Tommie's ears.

Somehow, the grandsons complied with Mr. Tommie's wishes and brought him a few limbs of what they believed to be shittam wood. Mr. Tommie set to work on his wood lathe that he housed in an old WWII Quonset hut out in the country. He turned the piece until he had a nice shape and began to sand it. His intention was to stain it to a fine finish, but, unfortunately, he had a massive stroke before he could complete his work. They found him in the hut one day and took him to the hospital. He survived the stroke, but the consequences were devastating as his speech was gone and most of his voluntary movement.

The baton for Mr. Welk was forgotten by everyone. As the grandchildren began the process of settling Mr. Tommie's estate, the time came to sell his property, including the country acre with the Quonset hut that he had used for storage for 40 years. The big pieces of equipment including the lathe were sold off one by one. A collection of pipes, wood, car parts, lawn mowers, and tools were sold or hauled away. Burn barrels were filled to the brim with scraps that were not deemed salvageable, and somehow, Mr. Welk's shittam wood baton found its way into the burn barrel and was lost.

Following his stroke and return home, the family turned on the TV every Saturday night so Mr. Tommie could watch the Lawrence Welk Show. As he watched the show, his eyes would water and he would try to conduct the band with his barely mobile right finger, emulating Mr. Welk and his baton. We believed he was telling us about the baton he made. It was one of the few times that family saw him "with us" before he passed.

The realization that we had accidently destroyed his baton was not something we shared with him. We allowed him to believe that Mr. Welk was using the baton he made for him. Was that a lie of omission or commission? A question we still face today.

MY MOTHER BUILT "CATHEDRALS"

"I am a firm believer that a teacher lives on and on through his students. I will live on if my teaching is inspirational, good, and stands firm for values and character training. Tell me how good teaching can ever die? Good teaching is forever, and the teacher is immortal."

Jesse Stuart, the famed Southern author's account of good teaching and its long-term value as quoted above served as a mantra for my late mother during her long teaching career in Huntsville, Alabama. As a mentor to students and aspiring teachers, she often succinctly defined teaching by using a simple, little story. The story began with an old man coming upon a construction site. Among the busy workers, he chose one and asked what he was doing. The worker replied that he was hauling bricks to make money to feed his family. The old man then approached a second laborer and asked the same question. The second laborer stated that he was mixing mortar because even though it was a hard, dirty job it was better than no job. The old man then approached a third laborer and asked the same question. The third man set his load of wood down, wiped his sweaty brow, and proudly proclaimed he was building a cathedral. As the old man walked away he thought all three laborers had valid answers to his question, but only the third man had a true vision of his task.

My mother possessed a true vision of her task as she practiced building "cathedrals" in a career of more than 35 years. The bricks she used were the essential skills of reading, language, history, etc. The mortar she used to bind the bricks and create a resilient structure was a mixture of personality, a genuine interest in and love for her students, and an indomitable expectation for success for all. The cauldron in which she mixed this binding mortar was great literature.

Students at Rison, Lee, and Huntsville High School were exposed to many great authors and pieces of literature, but one author, Jesse Stuart, was Mother's favorite. She first discovered Stuart as part of literary series at Alabama College. Mom was captivated by his exquisite physical descriptions, his well-developed, charismatic characters, the rhythmic ebb and flow of his language, and the positive moral threads that ran through the mostly fictionalized accounts of life among the indigenous people of the Appalachian Mountains. Stuart's tandem focus on education also captured her attention. She read all of his works and at some point acquired an autographed copy of *Hie to the Hunters*, which would play an important role in her life and the lives of her students.

It was in the cold winter of 1950 that Stuart's characters of Sparkie and Didway and the Plum Grove Hills first came to life for my brother and me. This duo of characters and their antics as depicted in *Hie to the Hunters* tells of an Appalachian, tobacco spitting teen who takes in a soft, runaway boy from a nearby town to help him escape bullying. Through daily work and play in the hills and hollows surrounding Sparkie's mountain home, the boys develop a deep and abiding friendship. This idyllic arrangement is threatened by Didway's parents' attempts to retrieve him, and the unrest between fox hunters and tobacco growers in the hills. Stuart masterfully embodied local color, dialect, exquisite descriptions, and compelling characters to illustrate a hardscrabble life.

After previewing the book with the home audience that winter, it traveled to school and was read to numerous classes and incorporated into math, English, reading, science, and writing lessons for many years to come. So impactful was this book that it almost became synonymous with my mother. At reunions, church services, and even her funeral, wherever former classmates were gathered, the conversation usually turned to Sparkie and Did, and was liberally punctuated with the squirting sound used to portray Sparkie's chosen weapon of defense, tobacco. From 1950 to her retirement in the late 1970s, many young Huntsvillians experienced this book and its inherent lessons as part of the building program.

About 20 years ago, I began a quest to find my Mom's well-worn copy of *Hie to the Hunters* to give to my brother. The book was out of print at the time, and eBay was not yet up and running, and as a last resort, I wrote the librarians at local schools asking if Mom had donated the book. I did not receive an answer for a long, long time, and had almost despaired of finding this treasure. Then, a few days before Christmas, the book appeared in my mailbox. With much anticipation, I gave the book to my brother. His reaction, as well as mine, was not unlike Sparkie's response to his Christmas present at the end of the book.

This past March, succumbing to full circle ideation, I used *Hie to the Hunters* to eulogize my brother, because in so many ways he was the honest, down to earth, fun-loving, moral Sparkie that he first encountered so many years ago. His life was one of Mom's beautiful "cathedrals" proving that good teaching by parent or professional never dies but lives on forever.

MEMORIES OF RISON SCHOOL

It's funny how the simple act of cleaning the attic and throwing away the detritus of a lifetime can transport you to another time and place. It happened to me the other day. As I sat on the attic floor rummaging through dusty old cardboard boxes, a lifetime of memories spilled out before me. There was the Shirley Temple doll, souvenirs from a class trip to Panama City, club awards, report cards, and some 45 RPM records. At the bottom of the box, I found a 1953 edition of the Pilot, the first yearbook published by Rison school. Turning the time worn, crinkly pages of that 65-year-old annual, I met face to face once again with teachers and friends from long ago. Fond remembrances of a time and place of innocence overtook me, and tears filled my eye.

Rison in 1953 was an intimidating structure that looked like a castle to a nine-year-old, especially when compared to the small, four room house in which my family lived. The building was huge and featured a red brick and green stucco exterior, giant banks of windows, and tall, arching entries with decorative insets. The columned entrance was impressive and featured a long sidewalk ending in matching white, marble water fountains. The bell cupola situated at the top in the middle of the school looked exactly like a turret from my fairy tale books. A chain length fence wreathed in honeysuckle vines surrounded the property and served, in my mind, as a moat to this castle. Wide interior halls with very high ceilings, oiled wooden floors that echoed every step, large cavernous classrooms with cloakrooms, an auditorium with a velvet curtained stage, and theatrical seats all contributed to a sense of grandeur for Rison.

As intimidating as the structure was, the playground was just the opposite. It was a beautiful open space perfect for running with the wind rushing through your hair. I was particularly fond of two huge, old oak trees that grew in the middle of the playground. Those trees were far enough apart that they made great bases for all kinds of tag games. We played freeze tag, swing statue, and partner chain tag using those trees. The swings were located at the back of the playground and the little kids always beat us to those at recess. The junior high kids always had a game going on the side nearest Oakwood. Next to the building you could find a group of kids playing wall ball, but only on the lower brick part of the facade as we had been admonished. Kids might be sitting there if they had committed an offense in which recess was denied. On pretty days, the teachers allowed us to spend our lunch hour on the playground instead of eating in the classrooms. Of course, we gobbled those sack lunches down to increase our play time. In the spring, I spent time viewing the biggest dogwood tree I ever saw at the house across the street from the school. My friend lived next door to that big tree and after school we played in the multitude of white blossoms that rained down and carpeted the ground. On windy days those beautiful blossoms sailed their way to our playground.

Rison was built in 1921. Prior schooling was conducted in a home on O'Shaughnessy Avenue and in the Moore residence which was given as the school site. The school primarily served the Dallas Cotton Mill population, and was named after Archie L. Rison, General Manager of the Mill. My family was not part of the Mill community, but we lived nearby, and since Mother taught at Rison, my brother and I were allowed to attend. Early on, Rison was a senior high school, but in 1953 it served as an elementary and junior high school, having released the upper grades to Butler

High School.

The yearbook stated a population of 142 junior high students and 275 elementary students in 1953. Class size varied significantly with some elementary grades having as many as 45 kids. Rison had a teaching staff of 17 with Mr. Cecil Fain as principal. The elementary teachers listed in the annual included Mrs. Kennamer, Miss Womack, Miss Essenlinger, Mrs. Taylor, Mrs. Pearson, Mrs. Ward, Mrs. Mellette, Miss Mitchell, Mrs. Lee, and Mrs. Pullen. Secondary teachers included Mr. Kennamer, Mr. Blackborn, Miss Harris, Mr. Randolph, Mrs. Graves, Mr. Myhand, Miss Monroe, and Mrs. Hanvey. Two other wonderful staff members were Mr. Beshears and Mr. Williamson, custodians, who would always return to school and unlock doors if you forgot your coat.

Rison quickly became home to my family as we attended all school-sponsored events. I loved all the carnivals, operettas, cake walks, and poetry readings as that meant opportunities for adventures which were quite limited in our lives. My first Halloween at Rison was truly special. I was the new kid and still a little uncomfortable. For days, all the kids talked about the costume they would wear for the school parade. I didn't have a costume, and the probability of getting one seemed unlikely. One day my dad came home with a big, square box and told me that would be my costume. I was not very excited until he told me about this new thing called television. Try as I might, I could not understand what television was, so he took me to Sears and showed me a TV set. I got excited as we started cutting a circle in front of the box to look like a television screen. Mom put waxed paper over the opening where my face was, and Dad created antennae for the top. I painted knobs on the sides. Dressed as a TV, I not only got honorable mention in the contest, but created great interest as most kids had never seen a TV. It would still be a few more years before we actually had one in our home.

I also remember a Christmas program presented by the fourth grade. All the girls had red dresses, carried holly rings, and danced in a circle singing *"Deck the Halls."* The next act was the fifth grade class singing *"Angels We Have Heard on High."* I had been chosen as one of the two angels to accompany this song, but getting out of the red dress and into my white costume proved very difficult. Despite Mother's help, I appeared late on stage as a much disheveled angel with a tilted wing and fallen halo.

Athletic events were central to our Rison experiences in 1953, as my brother played for the school. The junior football team, under Coach Myhand, had four wins and two losses ending the season with second place in the county league. Games were played at Rison's field. Team A basketball had a good season that year also, winning eleven games and losing only four. The B team won eight and lost six. Peewee teams in softball and baseball were also active, as well as the girls softball team. I remember the trophy case across from the school office had quite a collection of shiny awards.

World War II had only been over a few years in 1953, and Rison's continuing pride in their war efforts was noted in conversation and in the annual. Students were remembered for their assistance when a war-era, government sponsored Rationing Board was swamped with more work than they could manage. Rison people pitched in to help cover the load. The school also served as a location for issuing ration stamps. Sugar, meat, butter, silk, nylon, tires and other commodities were still in short supply as consumer production was slow to catch up following the War. Rubber was a particularly valuable commodity and a "victory" speed limit of 35 MPH was established to conserve tires and to operate within a four gallon a week gasoline ration for most people. For this reason, the majority of Rison students were still in the habit of walking to school, including my mother, brother, and me. As part of the War effort, Rison hosted scrap paper and metal drives as mentioned in the annual, and even at this late date following the War, evidence of that effort was still visible.

The greatest memories of my time at Rison revolve around the teachers covering the period of 1953-1958. Each teacher was unique and helped create a welcoming environment for kids. Mr. and Mrs. Kennamer set an example of a couple working together but demonstrating separate interests. Mr. Kennamer was a mathematician and scientist who valued higher level thinking skills. Mrs. Kennamer was a wonderful first grade teacher and managed the school store in which I worked as a student salesperson. I watched her kindness over and over as kids would be short a penny or two for purchasing a candy or a gum. She always made up the deficits personally. From her, I learned about compassion and charity.

Mrs. Mellette sparked my interest in art as she always used class murals depicting historical events in which research was more important than artistic ability. Mrs. Pullen started each day with reading from I Corinthians 13:13 inspiring love for each other. Mrs. Mitchell and Mr. Blackburn taught me to love theater and music, even though I had absolutely no talents in those areas. Getting Mr. Blackburn to play a jazz piece on the piano was a highlight. Miss Monroe taught proper English and appreciation of poetry. I remember a play in which my role was the Statue of Liberty. She taught me to portray that icon with pride. Mrs. Lee encouraged my love of literature. Mrs. Graves taught me about saving money and death, an odd combination. Her frugality was instilled in me because she would never spend a dime, so I would make certain her change was in dimes as much as possible. She often dramatically sang the verse, "Brother, can you spare a dime?" as she dropped her dimes in a metal bank. The lesson about death came late in my career at Rison. As my eighth-grade math teacher, I knew she was sick, but I had no idea she was terminal. My last memory of her was a visit with my mother to her hospital bed. At Mother's direction, I cut all of our beautiful blue and yellow Dutch iris' and arranged them in a vase for her. In that visit I realized my beloved teacher was dying, and I was inconsolable. Her gracious acceptance of her fate still lingers in my mind today.

The best teacher at Rison was my mother, Mrs. Hanvey, and I know I am prejudiced. I can't begin to delineate all she taught me. She was strict and demanded academic excellence, but she loved her students. It was not until her death in 1981 that

I realized the degree of positive impact she had on all her Rison kids as dozens of former students told wonderful stories on her. She epitomized the quality, character, and devotion of the teachers and staff at Rison that turned that austere castle into warm, inviting, and successful educational home. Those of us who attended Rison know first-hand just how lucky we were, and why, to this day, we still tear-up at the loss of a special time and place that was Rison School.

Repacking the attic boxes, I once again saved that old yearbook. Looking at the pictures of these people of yesterday, I can still hear their voices echoing in the halls as they greeted me each morning and called roll. I can see faces unaffected by the 65 years that have passed. I can, for only a moment, imagine that these vibrant people are all still with us, and I can imagine that Rison still stands at the corner of Andrew Jackson Way and Oakwood in Huntsville, Alabama.

THE SOUTHERN COTTON OIL MILL

A thunderous explosion on December 27, 1953 rattled the windows of our home in Huntsville, Alabama, and obliterated the post-Christmas reverie that we had been enjoying. The noise brought my entire family, as well as the neighbors, running outside late that cold evening. Something huge had blown up and it was close. Looking west from our home we saw a brilliant orange glow that lit up the entire north end of town, visible, I am sure, for many miles. My dad immediately suspected that his worksite, the Southern Cotton Oil Mill, was the likely source of the fire. We jumped into our car and sped toward Church Street. As we arrived, four fire trucks and about 30 firemen were already on the scene laying hoses. Dad stopped the car in front of the Mill office and ran headlong through a horde of onlookers onto the property. The fire chief caught him by the arm and they talked loudly for a few seconds before Dad and a fireman continued running to the back, right side of the property. Dad knew that one building, the old brick boiler room, was a major threat to the safety of the area because it was connected to the press room and only fifty feet from the fire. Adjacent to the boiler room were two huge storage tanks filled to capacity with the season's cottonseed oil awaiting shipment. My dad and the Chief understood the potential ramifications to the surrounding neighborhood if fire reached those tanks, either through a wind shift or if the valves and pipelines containing the oil were not closed. These pipelines would funnel fire directly to those storage tanks. Dad and the fireman successfully closed the oil valves, and fortunately, neither the tanks nor the boiler room exploded.

The fire was huge with flames leaping over a hundred feet in the air threatening all six large structures on the compound. Firemen used 4500 feet of hose and fought the fire for more than two hours before bringing the flames under control. In addition to the firemen's efforts, many people who lived nearby yielded themselves to the firemen's directions in handling hoses because the cotton products with their oils produced recurring hot spots over this three and a half acre area. Small homes around the perimeter of the Mill were doused with water as the sparks flew onto roofs. The Redstone Arsenal Fire Department shifted their coverage to the city as the Huntsville Department spent all local resources on this fire. Luck was also a player that night as a major shift in wind direction moved the fire away from the storage tanks.

The cause of the fire was never determined, but the origin seemed to be in the press room where eight hydraulic presses squeezed cotton seed into meal and oil. The plant was idle for the Christmas holidays, and of the nearly sixty employees, only the night watchman was on duty. He reported that he heard a blast and saw flames leaping from the press room. From there the fire spread to the adjoining buildings and two box cars which were located on a spur line that served the Mill. The fire was so hot that one of the box cars melted. Estimates of the damage ran between a quarter and half million dollars, even though the trademark, metal cotton seed storage houses, the frame warehouses, and the main office building were all spared.

In the morning paper, the Mill manager expressed the company's desire to rebuild a new, modern facility. He stated that rebuilding the old plant had been under consideration for some time. He further stated that this mill was termed a "low speed" plant that only processed about 250,000 tons of cottonseed yearly, and the remodeling would increase that capacity. He further stated that approximately 27,000 tons of product were saved so no shortage of cottonseed for spring planting was expected.

The Southern Cotton Oil Mill's history in Huntsville began in 1938. At that time Madison County, just like the rest of the country, was suffering from a terribly depressed economy. Huntsville's population was between 12,000 and 13,000 people. Nearly 76% of Huntsville's agricultural cash income came from cotton and cottonseed products, and 75% of non-farm income came from manufacturing cotton products. Fewer than seventeen industrial plants were operating within the city limits in 1938. The economic climate was right to capitalize on cotton products and with an available workforce in this location, the Southern Cotton Oil Mill of New Orleans established itself in Huntsville with the purchase of a small Alabama oil mill. The old Alabama Mill was located on the railroad depot property on Church Street. The original roundhouse was utilized for seed storage and a press room, and the railroad ticket office became the Mill office. From this humble beginning, the Southern Cotton Oil Mill grew significantly and became a major economic player in Huntsville operating continuously from 1938 until around 1985.

During the long and prosperous history of the Southern Cotton Oil Mill, cotton was truly "king" in this area. The Mill utilized and capitalized on virtually every aspect of this agricultural commodity, long before social movements prompted our collective conscience to become more conservative of natural resources. Products processed included lint, oil, meal, hulls, and, of course, seeds for planting.

Cotton shipped in from gins all over the area usually required three processing runs to remove the tightly compacted, fuzzy lint from the seed. Lint was the first product produced. Two processing runs were required to produce two different grades of lint. Those runs resulted in cotton bales that were shipped to various mattress companies who contracted with the Mill. The last processing run resulted in a very thin lint that was shipped to North Carolina where it was used for casing hot dogs and sausages.

Another product produced by the Mill was oil extracted from the cottonseed during the pressing process for meal. The oil was graded and sold to various companies for packing as cooking oil. The third product produced by the milling process was a thick, strong smelling meal that remained after the pressing of the oil. This product was responsible for the odor that permeated the entire north end of town. This very rich meal was mixed with crushed cotton hulls and sold for animal feed. And the last product was simply the residual hulls or meal that were sold as fertilizer to local farmers and gardeners.

Following the fire, a new company assumed ownership of the Mill for a number of years. The actual demise of the Southern Cotton Oil Mill came under the banner of progress. Development of the I-565 corridor, accompanied by the loosening hold of cotton on the area's economy, closed the chapter on this Huntsville business. Today, the old Southern Cotton Oil Mill site on Church Street is just a memory, a patch of clover, a parking lot, and a few structures under the overpass on I-565 between the Washington Street and Jackson Way exits. Surveying that piece of unpretentious ground, it is hard to realize that such a vibrant, important part of Huntsville's economic past once thrived there.

THE BRUSH ARBOR MEETING

Resting in the old, wooden swing on the front porch in the cool evening air after a long day's work in the fields, Grandad and I watched an old man approach on a mule across the bottom land near the creek. He was an old, Black man with hair as white as snow riding a mule that appeared almost as old as he was. Grandad recognized him at once, even from a distance, though his frame was painfully thin and his shoulders stooped. He had not seen him lately and had heard that his health was bad. In his prime, this man could pick 250 pounds of cotton a day and swing that canvas sack as if it was nothing.

Dressed in faded overalls with frayed legs and a torn bib pocket, the old man dismounted the swayback mule, petted his head, and gave him an apple. Supporting himself using the rock balustrades on the sides of the steps, he laboriously ascended our front porch. Grandad raised his hand in a gesture of hello and addressed him by the name of John. John responded with hand raised and hat removed and said, "Hello Cotton," as he ruffled my hair. Grandad motioned for John to sit in the rocking chair next to the swing and sent me in the house to get some sweet tea. John pulled a faded red bandana from his pocket and wiped profuse sweat off his brow. Grandad noticed a graying of his skin and a rattling of his breath.

I listened as the two men shared some pleasantries over a

glass of sweet tea. They talked of crops, the need for rain, and how it was good that cotton hoeing season was coming to an end. Vegetable harvesting had slowed a little too after the first rush of spring crops. They laughed about the bumper crop of purple hull peas expected this year by the profusion of blooms on the plants. Hopefully, now there would be a little more time available for other chores such as fence mending.

Refreshed by the sweet tea, the two old men continued reminiscing about the past. They talked about 1922, a bumper crop for cotton and corn, and how they didn't think they would get the crops in before the fall rains. They laughed about the snake that found its way into a woman's cotton-picking sack, and about the young kid who tried to put rocks in his sack to make it weigh more. They remembered riding mules with boards strapped across the mules' backs with cotton poison bags on each end that they would shake while making their way down each row of cotton. Grandad credited John with teaching him how to raise cotton, and how everyone depended on him when called up for service in World War I. Then John, in a more somber tone, began to talk about the seasons of his life; his childhood and the hardships he suffered when his parents died. He regretted his lack of schooling but was proud that he learned how to cipher numbers on his own. A sweet, toothless smile crossed his face when he talked about his late wife and his kids. Then John, in a halting whisper, asked Grandad if he knew Ecclesiastes 3:1-8. Grandad patted his Bible that was always beside him on the swing and began to recite, "To everything there is a season and a time for every purpose unto heaven."

John nodded his head and spoke of a last season he was approaching. Grandad understood he was here because he was dying. Was he just saying goodbye to an old friend? He had not seen him for a long time. In fact, the last time Grandad saw him was when he took a sack of turnips and a ham over to him last fall. John began again.

My season has done come. I been borned, I planted, and I done harvested everything. It's a fact, I laughed till I was near sick, and I done mourned and cried till I wist I was dead. Now my winter's acoming. I always knowed my purpose. I worked and put food on the table and a roof over my fambly's head. I knowed my job and I done it well, but I gots one more job to do. It come to me in a dream.

Grandad nodded his head at John's words. Recognizing the wisdom emanating from John's mouth, Grandad did not try to amend his statements, or speak platitudes about getting better. Instead he said, "My friend, what is it you wish of me?"

John went on to say that he had a dream of a great revival for his people; one like we had in the old days, but not a secret like it used to be. He expressed doubt in his family's salvation and felt his last purpose was to prepare them for eternity. He said, "They's good kids, but this here modern world don't leave 'em time to get right with Jesus." In his dream, he revisited a place of his youth before his parents died; the place where he was saved some 84 years ago. He called it a shade cathedral and his eyes shone as he talked about the place so filled with flowers, trees, sunlight, and the Lord's presence. He wanted to recreate that experience for family and friends. Explaining that they did not, as renters, have a piece of land on which to have this revival; he hoped his friend could help.

Grandad clarified what John was talking about was a brush arbor and went on to determine time and location. John had identified the location that he wanted. It was on the fringes of the bottom land near the creek which he had just crossed. Grandad knew the spot. It was a piece of low lying land covered in trees and shrubs that he had never cleared. It was virgin land with lots of spindly saplings and a few larger trees. John went on to tell Grandad that a circuit riding preacher would arrive in two days. Grandad agreed and John and his old mule slowly headed home.

The next day, Grandad took some picks and shovels along with his old mule team and harrow to clear a flat area with a path into the brush. While harrowing, several Black and white men came to help as the old man's idea had spread throughout the close community.

Once the area was cleared, several men identified some tall saplings that they could bend over and tie at the top with dried scuppernong vines to form a canopy. They lopped off any lower branches. Four larger trees having forks were identified near what would become corners of the arbor to hold additional limbs for support. With the skeletal shelter in place, Grandad chopped down some pine and cedar branches to make a canopy. Then he enlisted my help in gathering St. Peter's wreath and crepe myrtles branches from the plants that grew all around the house. These colorful branches were entwined in the canopy which made the interior of the arbor looks as if the ceiling was dripping red, white, and pink flowers with blossoms scattering to the soil below. The scent was so sweet. Several children from the community appeared with baskets of chains made by tying the white blooms of clover together. These were draped from the myrtle and St. Peter's branches so that they looked like little icicles. Roses, sweet peas, delphiniums, dahlias, and althea blooms were placed in old tin buckets all around the arbor. Lastly, a round, slick hickory stump was set up for a low pulpit. An assortment of benches, chairs, stools, and stumps for seating appeared as did pine torches for lighting.

Revival day came and everyone was keenly aware that John had not been seen during the process, nor had he offered any supervision as to how to build the brush arbor he remembered as a child. The arbor was ready, the preacher was on his way, gallon jars of sweet tea were ready, and a young girl had borrowed a pitch pipe for the singing. Concerned, friends and family went to John's house. There he sat under an old persimmon tree in his best overalls just waiting. With a smile on his face he explained that he wanted a Jericho march like in Joshua 6:1-27. With that he got his old arthritic limbs up and started hobbling toward the brush arbor saying, "Can't march no seven times 'round and don't want nothin' fallin' down, so instead of being silent we goin' march, we are goin' sing and sing loud!"

As the march started, Black and white people from the area joined. Upon arrival at the site, he lead the march around the arbor seven times singing, and then he sat down in a rocking chair with a soft cushion someone had provided.

The circuit riding preacher called the service to order. He began by explaining that Brother John wanted his family to experience revival in a setting as close to God as you can get. The preacher talked about the history of brush arbors as secret places for slaves of another time period to meet and worship. Awe inspiring Negro spirituals were born in places like these, and emotions in the arbor were not curtailed by masters. He further said these kinds of arbor revivals were dying, but Brother John was saved in just such a revival and one of his last wishes was that he wanted each of you to have the same opportunity.

Then the preaching and singing began. The preaching was strong, full of fire and brimstone, with calls for repentance before it was too late. It was an emotional evening that continued late into the night. Many people wept and accepted Christ as their savior. Several were baptized in the cool water of the creek behind the arbor. After much praying, preaching, and singing John stood up and asked the congregation for a "laying on of hands." He explained that his time on earth was almost done and he wanted his friends' prayers for him as he prepared to join his wife in heaven. He also stated that his death was to be a time of celebration and no grieving. He extolled everyone to just sing praises to the Lord.

As the service ended and the pine torches extinguished, two men in the congregation formed a seat by crisscrossing arms to carry John home. He left singing the old spiritual, "I'll Fly Away," at the top of his voice. As Grandad and I watched, he commented that this little piece of ground had been sanctified by this worship service, and as sacred ground, it would never be cleared for farming; and it never was.

The old man was right; his season on earth came to an end not long after the brush arbor experience. We attended his service and, just like he wanted, it was a joyous celebration. He left this life with the confidence that he provided the people he loved an unforgettable experience in which Christ's salvation was offered and received by many. Not only was his season on earth finished, but his purpose accomplished. Would that we all could be as clear in purpose as he was. I can imagine he was received by the Lord with the words so desired by us all ". . .well done my good and faithful servant."

TREASURE ON BILLY GOAT HILL

That April morning broke warm and humid with dark, rumbling clouds building to the west of Billy Goat Hill. The neighborhood boys planned to meet my brother at the vacant lot next to our house for pitching and batting practice before an afternoon baseball game. As the boys gathered it was clear that their moods matched the gloom of the day. They knew instinctively that the game would be called due to inclement weather, and that their mothers would call them home early as a weather precaution.

With the prospect of an impending storm and a boring Saturday, four teenaged boys leaned against the back fence, grumbling and waiting for the inevitable call home. "Birds on a wire" was the term my Dad used to describe them as he viewed their posture and attitudes. I can still see those "birds" dressed alike in dark blue jeans with razor sharp creases and turned up cuffs, white-shirts with the sleeves rolled up a couple of times, and black, high top tennis shoes with long, white laces. Greased slicked back hair and the proper, disdainful James Dean look completed the picture.

The boys stood adjacent to a long, bare strip of soil in our yard devoid of any grass or weeds, not even spring dandelions. That naked strip of ground, the uncovered pipe in the ground, and the shiny, three-foot-tall spigot was evidence of a new city water line just recently installed by Dad. A central access line was provided to neighborhoods by the city, but residents were responsible for extending the line to their own property. The access line was located more than 300 feet from our house and digging the ditch to contain the water line had been back breaking and time consuming, but finally, we had water in the backyard, not yet in the house. That would take another year to gather the finances to install indoor plumbing. Water in the backyard meant we no longer had to carry all of our water from the street behind the house.

Dad spent weeks digging a trench through hard, red clay to lay pipe, and Mom scrimped and saved to buy the pipes. After completing the trench line and positioning pipes, our yard was left with large, sunken places, and the pipes needed a layer of dirt to keep them from freezing in the winter. Those sunken areas were dangerous as we still had to carry buckets of water to the house and wash bench, and baskets of clothes to the clothes lines over those open areas.

On the Friday evening preceding the Saturday my brother and his friends were going to play baseball, Dad had a friend deliver a truck load of fill dirt and cottonseed hulls which he dumped parallel along the pipeline ending in front of the back porch door. Dad had planned on a pretty spring day and some help to move the dirt into place. Now, with the anticipated change in weather, it appeared that he was faced with the task of moving this mound of dirt quickly before the rains turned it into a pile of mud.

Dad came over and sat down beside me on the old, wooden wash tub bench where I was petting my cat. "Do you think the 'birds' will help me spread this dirt?" I just laughed because I knew he was kidding. Even as Dad got up, all the boys conveniently turned away, pretending not to see him or the potential task. "They're going to spread all this dirt and I won't even have to ask them or say one word to them about it. Do you believe me, Chica? Just watch."

From my spot on the bench, I watched Dad pick up a

shovel and began to spread the dirt on an area of exposed pipe near where the boys were standing. Suddenly with exaggerated motions, he reached over and picked something shiny up from the dirt. He blew on it, wiped it on his pants, and slipped it in his pocket. Then he went back to spreading shovels of dirt. He had his back to the "birds." He stopped again, picked something up, blew on it, and put it in his pocket.

Slowly, the boys' curiosity got to them and they sauntered over. Dad never turned around, but he looked at me and winked. Whistling, he picked something up again, blew on it, and tossed it to me. Soon all the boys found the extra shovels that just happened to be placed against the house and started digging. Suddenly, one of the boys yelped as he found a coin, blew on it, and put it in his pocket. Dad moved over to the bench where I was sitting as the boys dug furiously into that long pile of dirt racing to be the first in an untouched area. Those oh so clean, "birds" ended up a mess as they quickly figured out the faster they dug the more coins they found. That pile of dirt was spread within record time and completed just as it started to sprinkle and moms called kids home. Each boy left cheerfully whistling and jingling money in his pocket. They had found an unexpected treasure on Billy Goat Hill.

After Dad raked a 2x4 over the dirt to smooth it, I watch as he deftly scattered grass seeds. It became clear to me that Dad had seeded the dirt with coins while it was being unloaded the night before. When I asked him why he had planted coins in the dirt pile he smiled and said,

> It's as plain as the nose on your face, Chica. If you want corn, you plant corn kernels. If you want grass, you plant grass seeds. If you want initiative, you plant incentive in the heart or mind. No matter how much you fuss or gripe or prod, you can't ever make grass or corn grow. It's the same with people. Pushy words may get the job done for you, but the result will be resentment, not initiative, and initiative should always be the goal.

Many years later, I found myself in a college child psychology class. The professor asked for positive examples of molding children's behavior, and I immediately thought of Dad and his Billy Goat Hill treasure. My classmates and professor listened in awe as I explained the magic that Dad worked with his "birds on a wire." As I pondered anew his wisdom, I realized that the real treasure on Billy Goat Hill was my Dad.

GOT GOAT?

In 1957, a young professional man from Maryland secured a new job working for Thiokol in Huntsville, Alabama. His project was at the Redstone Arsenal working on the T-18 Falcon Missile Project which would eventually become the world's first solid fuel rocket system. The engineer, whose name has been lost in the retelling of this story, along with his wife and three children, struggled financially through his long college education, but this new job held the promise of material dreams for the first time in their married life. Their dream was living a rural, wholesome life surrounded by nature.

After arriving in Huntsville, they purchased a "farmette" with a wonderful, ranch style house on an acre of land for a hefty $13,000.00. They also purchased their first new car, a 1957 Colony Park Station Wagon, Nantucket blue with fake wood trim for $3,000.00.

In hunting for their "farmette," the family visited almost all of the outlying areas around Huntsville. They marveled at the beauty of the mountains, valleys, and wildlife. Their real estate agent sent them to view many properties, but one particular property and its owner impressed the whole family and brought them back again even after purchasing their "farmette."

This property might have been right out of the Progressive Farmer magazine or a staged picture postcard. The view consisted of an old clapboard farmhouse set against a breathtaking backdrop of nature, petunias cascading from the rails of the front porch, and a grandfatherly old man with a straw hat, a white beard and overalls napping in the swing. A return visit was required, so they went one Saturday afternoon. Just as they walked up the steps to the porch, a little white goat bleated and popped its head up from the old man's lap. Following the many oohs and aahs from the children, the old man began to put Babe, the little white nanny goat, through her entertainment paces. On command, Babe got candy out of the old man's pocket, drank from his tea glass, nuzzled against his cheek when he asked her for a kiss, and put her head in his lap when he told her to nap. The children fell in love with this little goat and wanted Dad to buy it for them, but Babe was not for sale.

The trip home was sorrowful! The children cried because they wanted that little goat. The father thought the children would eventually forget about the goat and things would settle down.

After a week of crying, Dad told Mom to find a goat. Mom searched the want ads and finally went to the Farmers' Market where she found a goat for sale ad on the bulletin board. She called her husband very excited with the news and told him she was taking the children to find the goat that was somewhere near New Hope. She asked him how much she should pay for a goat. Her husband's somewhat agitated response was, "Just get a goat. I don't care how much it costs! I don't care what color it is or anything else! Just don't come home without a goat! I can't stand to hear the kids cry anymore!"

Mom, in her matching yellow pedal pushers and shirt, polished nails, make-up, and smooth pageboy hairdo piled into that beautiful Mercury station wagon and headed off toward New Hope. They were singing and laughing and trying to think of a name for the new goat. After a few wrong turns and several stops for directions, they finally found their way to a rather dilapidated, remote house with a sign in the yard that said, "Goats for Sale."

Despite some misgivings, Mom knocked and a gnarly man

opened the door and invited them in. The price of the goat was $25.00, and a real bargain according to the man. As they exited the front door, Mom asked where the goat was and he pointed toward the back yard. He told her that the goat was chained because it liked to eat his vegetables. He also told her to take the chain and the lock with her, and then he went back into the house and closed the door rather abruptly.

The children raced to the back yard with Mom close behind. Suddenly, they stopped. There stood the meanest looking, ugliest Billy goat you could imagine. Mom, not being well-versed in goat anatomy or disposition, encouraged the kids. "I'm sure she will look much better when we get her home and give her a bath. Shampoo and cream rinse will do wonders. Let's get her in the car."

They walked toward that Billy goat, who never took his eyes off of them. As Mom slipped the key into the lock and unwrapped the chain from around the pole, she kept one eye on the chain and one on the goat. Once the chain was loose, that goat took off rearing up on its hind legs showing himself to be nearly as tall as she was. As she began to pull that goat toward the car, she yelled at the kids to open the back doors. She pushed and pulled and finally got the goat to the car. She crawled into the rear seat backwards and pulled that goat in after her. Then she yelled at the kids to close the back door in which they had entered while she exited the back door immediately behind her rear. In all the commotion to close the doors, no one noticed that the goat had lunged at the window and knocked himself out cold. Mom thought he had just settled down and gone to sleep. With kids and goat in the car, Mom headed back to Huntsville quite proud of her accomplishment.

Somewhere just south of Monte Sano Mountain on Highway 231, the goat regained consciousness. He went bezerk! He started jumping back and forth from the back seat to the rear of the station wagon and bleating wildly. Mom pulled that beautiful Mercury over to the side of the road and everyone, except the goat, bailed out. The Billy goat was possessed was what Mom would later write on the insurance report. That goat continued to jump back and forth between the seats, and the faster he jumped the more that chain and the attached combination lock flailed about. Whap, the chain hit the back window and it cracked. Whap, the rear-view mirror came off! Whap, the door handle sailed into the side window and it cracked!

Mom and the three children ran to a service station to call her husband. She told him she had abandoned the car, called a taxi to take them home, and to go get that car. Before he could determine what happened, she added a comment reminiscent of what he had said to her earlier, "And you had better come home with that goat. I have not come this far to have you quit in the face of a little adversity!" Several kindly observers offered assistance. It was obvious by this very attractive lady's appearance and demeanor that she had a problem. Her pageboy hairdo had gone limp, those pretty yellow pedal pushers were dirty, she had lost a shoe, and her voice was just a shade shy of hysterical.

When the husband arrived, he found his state-of-the-art new Mercury in shambles. The seats were ripped, all the windows were cracked, the covers on the gauges were broken, and there was a terrible odor emanating from the car. That Billy goat was standing in the back seat chewing part of the front seat, with his wife's shoulder bag hanging from one horn. The goat was still only because he had wrapped that chain around so many obstacles that no slack remained. The man surveyed the situation before a watchful audience of curious bystanders. He decided he could drive the car home since the steering wheel and gear shift remained intact and the goat was unable to move.

Upon arriving at his home, the husband hauled that goat out to his backyard, none too tenderly. He secured the goat's chain around a wooden post in front of the well house. After listening to his wife's account of the story, the man called his insurance agent and said, "You aren't going to believe what happened to my brand new car!?"

Dad, thoroughly disgusted with the situation, issued an ultimatum, the goat has to go! The kids started crying saying that the goat would get better. They believed he could be trained to be gentle and loving like Babe. Mom said she was not ready to give up after all she had gone through to get that goat home. Dad knew that an old, cranky Billy goat could never be trained to be the right kind of pet for his children, but how to get rid of this goat without crossing his wife and children was another matter. Every day the goat and the man disliked each other even more. The man was determined that the goat, pardon the pun, would not get his goat! He decided he would just bide his time and the answer would come.

The Billy goat had been part of the family for about a week when Dad went outside to mow the grass. The goat, standing on top of the wellhouse, glared at him. The man began making cutting sweeps on his yard, cursing that goat under his breath. After a few sweeps, he noticed that the goat was moving backwards as every sweep of the mower brought him closer to the well house. Each time the mower crossed directly in front of the well house, the man would rev the engine causing the goat to forcefully jump backwards. This went on for quite a while, and a potential solution to the problem of the goat formed in the man's mind. As his cutting sweeps moved closer and closer, the goat moved farther and farther back on the well house and away from the post putting more tension on the chain. Suddenly, the man gave a loud, evil laugh and cut the engine quickly causing the mower to backfire loudly. The goat jumped and fell off the back of the well house, and the post broke. With a chuckle and a look of total satisfaction, the man spun his mower around toward the front of the yard as the goat raced into the woods dragging the chain and post with him. He was never seen again.

The young engineer began to recite an old Finnish saying someone at work had been teasing him with since the goat arrived, "If you are short of trouble, take a goat!" Right then and there, he decided to forgo all goats and surprise his family with an irresistible, cuddly puppy instead.

THE SPARROW

In 1961, Alabama was in the midst of the Civil Rights' Movement, an era that fostered the best and worst of human behavior. Heroic efforts to chip away at long-standing, segregationist policies were chronicled daily by news media. Less visible, but no less heroic, were the personal campaigns of benevolence that many temperate Black and white citizens practiced mitigating the rancor of the day and find common ground on which to build relationships. This is the story of one of those relationships, a chance encounter of two rather insignificant people who were powerless to change well-entrenched Southern social order or affect major changes in political structures. Instead, this single meeting resulted in one individual's expression of humanity to another and the recipient of that humanity being changed forever.

As a 17-year-old college freshman, I traveled by bus from my home in Huntsville, Alabama to Birmingham where I changed busses to continue on to Montevallo where I attended Alabama College. Late one Sunday afternoon as I arrived in Birmingham, I found myself in the middle of a Civil Rights' demonstration. I sat down quietly on the wooden benches that lined the walls of the waiting room and began to study while I awaited my bus. From this vantage point, I watched the demonstrators, as I had on several occasions before. According to the placards, today's demonstration was against the city commissioners and their threats to close the bus station cafeteria if Blacks and whites were allowed to eat together.

Suddenly, several young Black men burst into the waiting area. These men appeared to have an agenda focused on civil disobedience. They harassed the demonstrators, physically and verbally. Some of the demonstrators attempted to quell the situation by suggesting that the unruly men leave, or else join the peaceful demonstration. At that suggestion one of the men uttered a string of expletives and knocked an older man down. Tensions were escalating.

As the shouting increased, I became aware that I was the only person other than the demonstrators and the unruly men left in the waiting room. The ticket agents and other passengers left. Previously, I had gone unnoticed, but now several of the rowdy men began moving toward me cursing angrily. I was petrified.

From out of nowhere, an old, Black gentleman in a neatly pressed uniform appeared. He was white-headed, hunched over, and frail; yet strength and dignity emanated from him. Fearlessly, he shuffled through the crowd. His very presence seemed to still the chaos, and, as if on command, those angry young men parted in unison as he made his way toward me. His eyes, clouded with age, were intense and never veered from mine. After what seemed an eternity, he stood before me, and held out a leathery hand with fingers like long, brown gnarled twigs. Instinctively, I knew I could trust him. I took his hand and together we walked through that crowd; a crowd that turned and followed us. Oh, we must have been an amusing sight, a study in contrast. He was small, Black, old and gray, and I was tall, white, young and blonde.

We walked over to a dimly lit room that opened onto both the waiting area and a back hall. The old man motioned for me to sit down on a metal chair as he exited the back door. The room was obviously the custodian's closet. Brooms, mops, cleaning supplies, and pictures of children and pets appointed the area. A few minutes later, the gentleman reappeared with a crumpled, brown paper bag and wet paper towels. He slowly wiped his hands on one towel and gave me one to do the same. He sat down in the chair opposite me, opened the brown bag, and took out the contents. Waxed paper held a sandwich which he meticulously halved, placing one part on my napkin and one on his. The he cut an apple and did the same. Next, he poured half of a warm Double Cola into a Dixie cup. He took my hands again and we said grace as our audience watched in silence. As we shared his bologna sandwich, the irony of the situation was conspicuous, as were the incredulous stares of the crowd observing the scene.

I asked the old gentleman about the pictures I presumed were grandchildren. He grinned proudly and told me about each one. One attended the University of Chicago, another played piano at the church, and one was in the U.S. Army. Then he asked me where I was going to school and what I was studying. I told him Alabama College, and that I wanted to become a teacher like my mother and grandmother before me. He nodded and said that was a noble task. We whiled away an hour or so eating supper and sharing bits and pieces of our lives, this stranger and me. We watched our audience disperse a few at a time without comment. Finally, he pulled out his pocket watch and remarked that my bus was on time.

The old gentleman escorted me to my bus, although the unruly men had vanished. I thanked him again and asked why he had helped me. In the most benign manner he answered, "God heard his sparrow's cry and He sent me." The simplicity and radiance of his face left an indelible mark on my heart.

I waved as my bus pulled away, and immediately regretted not having asked his name. Somehow, even in youthful innocence, I knew I had experienced a defining moment in my life. And, as darkness enveloped my bus that evening, the old man's benevolence enveloped my thoughts and found a place in my future. I knew then, that as a teacher, I would always seek out the troubled sparrows in my classroom, and in fond remembrance of my docent of humanity, intervene with simple kindness.

ANOTHER TIME, ANOTHER PLACE

Jo Ellen's mother died! Friends gathered around her on the cold, linoleum floor surrounding the phone booth in the dormitory hall late one evening while she talked to her father and cried inconsolably. A senior dorm advisor, who had family in northern Alabama, was summoned to drive Jo Ellen home. I quickly agreed to go with them, and after packing a few things for both of us, we set off for an experience and a people that would leave an indelible impression on me.

Jo Ellen and I had become friends, not just roommates, in the weeks since we met as college freshmen. Intuitively, we recognized vast differences in our backgrounds and experiences. She came from a remote mountain community that had no real name, and I came from the modern city of Huntsville, well on its way to becoming America's Space Capital in 1961.

The three of us headed north in a little Volkswagen, driving for what seemed an eternity through a darkness so thick that you could almost cut it. Jo Ellen was stony silent, and we respected her solitude. As we neared Scottsboro, she began to give complicated directions to her home. It was dawn by the time we left the blacktopped highway for the chert rocked road and then to a well-worn logging trail before finally reaching their farm.

A small, clapboard farmhouse backed up against a mountain ablaze with fall colors was the first thing I saw as the early morning sunlight dissolved the darkness. I noticed several wagons with mule teams, one old rusty truck, and dozens of people moving about. The sound of our car's motor broke the quiet morning and attracted everyone's attention. As the car stopped, Jo Ellen bolted out and melted into her dad's waiting arms. I grabbed our things and made plans with the senior dorm advisor for the return trip. Watching that little Volkswagen disappear down that logging trail in a cloud of dust, I had an uneasy feeling that I had somehow been transported to a place very different than I had ever been before, even though I knew it was only a few miles from my home in Huntsville.

Jo Ellen introduced her father, a tall, wiry man with a head full of wavy, black hair graying at the temples. His flannel shirt and overalls hung loosely from his shoulders, and a brisk breeze whipped his pants back and forth against his obviously bony legs. On his feet were dust-covered, rolled-over brogan shoes. He was surrounded by an odd assortment of people who introduced themselves and offered sincere hugs. Taking our suitcases, they wrapped their arms around Jo Ellen and me and guided us to the house.

The first thing I saw was the front door draped in a long, black flowing cloth. A crisp breeze brushed against that cloth making it appear to tremble. Standing on the rock porch steps, the view into the front room was unobstructed. At the threshold of the door, a thick line of salt was mounded which I later learned was to keep evil spirits from entering the house of the deceased. Another black cloth was draped over the fireplace mantle covering a large mirror and a clock that had been stopped at the time of death. And, even though it was quite chilly, every window in the house was open so that the spirits could roam free.

As we stepped into the room, I saw Jo Ellen's mother laid out on a wooden door anchored by two straight, ladder backed chairs. She was dressed for burial in a white dress with long sleeves, a crocheted collar, and a thin ribbon bow at her throat. Her hands were folded together across a tiny waist and a crude cross made of two sticks was tucked inside her hands. In the middle of her chest was a saucer with what appeared to be equal measures of salt and earth, representing spirit and body. Her long, black hair was piled up in a bun.

As Jo Ellen entered the parlor, a group of women enveloped her. One old matron who was obviously in charge wrapped her arms around Jo Ellen and started a one-sided conversation with her,

Honey, we couldn't wait fer you to dress her. This here is the dress she'd have wanted, I think. You know we cleaned her real good. I washed and oiled her hair and put in my lacquered barrette to keep it from coming undone. You know we'd have waited fer you if we could, but we couldn't cause she would have gone stiff and we couldn't have fixed her purty. And we put silver nickels on her eyes, and kept her face fresh looking with a baking soda and water poultice. You all right, honey?

Jo Ellen nodded. Then an old man came up to her and said,

Jo, Baby, the coffin's gonna be here real soon. The Mitchell Boys is a makin' it. I done told them to make it out of good poplar wood and varnish it, tho' it takes longer. Your momma would've liked it better that way. Now when it gets here, we gots some nice cloth we gonna line it with.

Jo Ellen had not yet said a word.

There was no real discussion as to why this young woman died. I did overhear conversations regarding Jo Ellen's mother's sudden and severe weight loss. Apparently, she just passed out washing dishes. Someone went down to the store and called a doctor, but she was dead before the phone call was made. I also heard bits and pieces about how her husband and hired hand laid her on the ground so that the mysterious forces of death were in touch with the mysterious forces of earth.

In a soft voice, Jo Ellen asked if the bell had been rung. Jo

Ellen and her father went out to the front porch where a large, metal dinner bell hung. She grasped the rope and her dad gently wrapped his hand around hers. Together, they rang the bell 34 times, one for each year of her mother's life. The sound of the tolling bell echoed on the crisp autumn air. I watched as men off in the distance stopped the grave digging and removed their hats as the bell tolled its poignant tale of death.

In preparation for the wake, neighbors began arriving with arm loads of materials and food. Makeshift tables of saw horses and long planks covered with checkered oil cloths held fried chicken, sausage, ham, green beans, boiled potatoes, corn, rutabagas, greens, turnips, and all kinds of cakes and pies. While the ladies dealt with the food, the men removed furniture from the parlor, swept it clean, and arranged straight chairs around the walls. Despite the hustle, someone always sat with the body and prayed orally or recited Bible verses.

The simple wooden coffin arrived in two separate pieces, a bottom and a flat lid. It was varnished to a light caramel color. As men sat the coffin up on straight chairs, several ladies ran their rough, weathered hands along the structure admiring the quality of workmanship.

A man brought in a half–full canvas cotton picking sack. Jo Ellen and the old woman in charge began filling the inside of the coffin with fluffy, white cotton bolls. "We're makin' a nice bed fer your Momma," she said rather matter-of-factly. She kept rearranging the cotton bolls where the head would lie. "Don't want your Momma's neck to crimp," she whispered. A white lining fabric was tacked inside to cover the cotton bolls. Once the old matron was satisfied, she informed the men that the coffin was ready.

Several men lined up on either side of the body, and very carefully picked it up and laid it in the coffin. The old woman made sure that the dress, which had been split in the back for ease in dressing the body, did not open and compromise modesty. With the body in place, Jo Ellen lovingly straightened her mother's collar and bow, smoothed the dress about her, and swept wispy hairs from her forehead. People quietly exited for this private moment between mother and daughter.

As I stood on the front porch trying to find my composure in the face of such a stark reality, a reality with which I had no experience and did not comprehend, a young sprite of a girl took my hand and we ran off to gather wild flowers. We picked bunches of purple October flowers and goldenrod. We passed men coming from the woods with fall colored branches of red sumac, golden maple, and maroon dogwood, as well as cedar, pine, and holly.

Suddenly, the young girl started talking. "I knowed last week that grief was acomin' to us. I done heered an old barn owl hoot three times as I was a comin' home from church last Sunday night. That's a bad omen you know!" She continued justifying the grief she knew was coming by talking about other signs and future events revealed in her coffee grounds. She told how her grandma's rocking chair just start rocking for no reason, and how she heard the dogs howling in the night. All omens of future grief she assured me. I didn't put much stock in what she was saying, but I kept quiet.

Back at the house, the men placed the tree branches with the colorful leaves, bright berries, and greenery under the coffin. We put tall stalks of colorful hollyhocks into large earthenware pickle crocks and placed them at either end of the coffin. Mason jars full of wild flowers were placed on the window sills around the parlor. The old matron surveyed the premises with her keen eye and declared that the house was ready.

More people came to the house, on foot, on horseback, and in wagons. Many carried musical instruments, chairs, plates, silverware, and more food. They came to the front parlor and knelt in prayer by the deceased. Many kissed her on the cheek, but all touched her in some way. After paying their respects, they mingled in and out of the house, hovering around Jo Ellen and her dad. The old matron invited everyone to a repast.

After the breaking of bread, a man with a booming bass voice stood up and started singing. Everybody joined in singing or playing instruments to songs such as "In the Sweet Bye and Bye," "Swing Low, Sweet Chariot," or "Love Lifted Me." Singing and speeches about Jo Ellen's mother filled the parlor until late that night. Little children were put down on quilts, and old ones with bones likely to stiffen up in the cold night air were taken home to sleep in their own beds. Most of the men and women stayed to sit up all night with the body.

With morning, a circuit riding preacher arrived by car and the funeralizing began. A line of people formed and walked by the body, again touching her and saying special words of love or stating remembrances of joyful times together. Lastly, Jo Ellen and her dad came to view the body. When they sat down, the preacher started the service. He talked about what a good woman she was, and how the Lord calls some home early. He talked about the trials and tribulations here on Earth and admonished the congregation to be prepared to meet their maker at any time. With each statement, loud deep-voiced "amens" came from all around the parlor. Then the preacher read from the Bible about the worth of a Christian woman. We sang some songs and prayed. A wobbly, old man gave the final amen and led all of us out into the front yard. As Jo Ellen and her dad stepped out on the porch, I heard the coffin being nailed shut. With each nail I shuttered, as if the finality of this death was being driven home. A woman standing next to me put her arm around my shoulder. I did not resist.

The coffin was transported to the burial site in an old wagon decorated with colorful fall leaves and pulled by a team of mules. Jo Ellen and her dad, tall, erect, and stoic, walked behind the wagon. Neighbors filed in behind singing and shouting Bible verses as they walked to the family cemetery. Just beyond the cemetery's low rock wall, a group of men stood at attention, waiting for the body, hats and shovels in hands. The coffin was unloaded from the wagon and carried around the grave three times. That was the apparent signal for something called keening to begin. The old matron began a sort of high pitched wail about Jo Ellen's mother as she moved from grave to grave in the little family plot. Much of what she said I could not understand, but it seemed to be a loud song acknowledging the deceased's family and her good deeds. Several women responded in a chorus. The coffin was then placed on a bed of ropes across the open grave. The preacher continued his comments and a few more songs were sung. Then, the young men using the ropes and working in rhythm lowered the coffin into the ground. Jo Ellen and her dad scooped shovels of dirt and let them reluctantly slide into the grave. Everyone shoveled dirt on to the coffin, and the ladies threw wild flowers they had gathered during the procession.

Following the burial, people returned to the house to eat again. The women spent most of the rest of the day cleaning up. The men sat on the porch, and, in an unplanned show of comradeship, whittled with their knives. Jo Ellen and her dad walked and talked. They visited the burial site again and swept it clean with a cedar branch.

The next morning, a group of women returned to clean the house. It was unclear why so young a woman had died, so the women decided to scrub the house in case it was a contagious sickness. They also boxed the woman's personal effects for storage. The men, including Jo Ellen's dad, went back to work in the fields. There was hay to be made and cotton to be picked before the weather turned bad.

The senior woman who brought us north returned. After loading the car, we stopped a ways down the path from the house where Jo Ellen's father was picking cotton. There, the two of them said good-bye. As the three of us headed back to college, we didn't talk at all. Each of us was lost in our own thoughts. Jo Ellen cried softly, and my heart ached for her. I placed a pillow on my lap and motioned for her to put her head down. Exhaustion and the motion of the car claimed her and she surrendered to sleep.

Back on the main highway with its fast-moving traffic and commercial enterprises and back in the 20th century to which I was accustomed, the full significance of the experience began to hit me. I realized that I had been privy to another time and another place, existing adjacent to my world and yet, not in my world. I had experienced one of life's hardest moments, death, with a people who on the surface appeared utterly simple and superstitious, but in reality, demonstrated a wisdom and reverence for life that still impacts me fifty years later.

NOT ME!

"Not me!" is a frequently heard childhood refrain that serves to declare a blameless state. Those two little words are used to release one from responsibility, participation, causation, and results. Taken literally, it means, I didn't commit the infraction or I'm innocent; however, in Birmingham, Alabama in 1963, that little childish phrase served to indict me for indifference and change me forever.

I was in my last year of college in 1963 and I could literally see the light at the end of a long tunnel. As part of the first group of three teaching candidates, the college allowed me to go to Birmingham to student teach. I was 19 years old. I had a wonderful mentor teacher and great second grade students. The college, in an effort to protect its co-eds, required student teachers to live with a family. My friend's parents graciously offered to house me for the semester. Their other daughter and her two children also lived with us. I did not have a car, but like lots of people in Birmingham at the time, I rode a city bus everywhere I went. I loved Birmingham and my new-found freedom.

On Sunday mornings I rode a bus to First Baptist Church on North 6th and 27th Streets in downtown Birmingham. The two children of my friend's sister, ages seven and nine, often went with me to Sunday School and worship services. The fall morning of September 15, 1963 was just such a day. We left early to catch a bus for Sunday school, and once there, I walked each child to class and then joined my class.

In the opening coffee and comments before the start of my class, there was much banter about the civil unrest in Birmingham. This past summer's wave of violence and accusations as to responsibility dominated the men's conversation. "Bull" Connor, sheriff, was either praised or condemned for using water hoses and dogs to quell the student demonstration at Kelly Ingram Park. There was also heated talk from proponents and opponents of George Wallace, Governor of Alabama, an outspoken segregationist. Names, unfamiliar to me, were mentioned including Martin Luther King Jr., Ralph Abernathy, and Fred Shuttlesworth. In the middle of this chatter, an older man unexpectedly turned and questioned me. "Do you have any views on this situation, young lady?"

My response was, "Not me." I did not want to add to the conversation simply because I had nothing to say and did not want to show my ignorance regarding current events. Politics held no interest for me. No episodes of unrest had been experienced in my college town, and with very limited access to news coverage either by TV or newspaper, I was abysmally uninformed. I continued to listen to this discussion in a distant, "Not me," manner because even though the conversation made me uncomfortable, it did not directly concern me. I was relieved when class started.

The Sunday school lesson that beautiful fall morning was on the First Epistle to the Corinthians from the New Testament, chapter 13. I'm not sure why I remember the subject of the lesson that day except my 5th grade teacher started every day with that Bible selection; maybe, my mind traveled back in time to her words about faith, hope, and love. In retrospect and in light of the coming events of the day, I found the lesson quite ironic, but, of course, at that time on that fateful Sunday morning I had no idea of just how ironic.

Class ended about 10:00 am. As usual, I went to get my

friend's niece and nephew to go to "big" church as First Baptist Birmingham was a large, imposing structure. I retrieved both children and suddenly heard a booming noise. Instantly, I knew something was terribly wrong. Without hesitation, I grabbed the children's hands and ran out of the church by the nearest exit, thinking something had happened at the church. Standing on the sidewalk amidst a like-minded crowd of people, it was eerily silent. An acrid smell scented the air. Then out of the silence came the sounds from multiple sirens. Church members who had previously stood in silence pondering the situation began to talk nervously, distraught and afraid, trying to determine exactly what happened. One man commented that a gas line must have exploded somewhere, or else it was an accident at one of the steel mills. Another said he thought he heard gunfire. Smoke was billowing off to my right, and cars were stopping in the middle of the street and people were exiting. Voices of far off anger began to invade my consciousness and a fear rose in my gut. I felt trapped by the multitude of people milling about the sidewalks exuding a collective fear. The flight instinct took over. I had to get away from the church and that unknown thing that was happening.

With kids in tow, I hurried to our usual bus stop, but the police surrounded it. I wasn't sure the bus could even get to the stop. So we ran two blocks to see if another bus might have a better chance of making its stop. It looked promising since it was clear of police presence, but more and more emergency vehicles were speeding to the site. Finally, the bus came and we boarded. The route was blocked, and the driver had to U-turn as directed by the police. The detour put us within sight of the 16th Street African-American Baptist Church, and the area we just left. It was obvious the church was the scene of something horrific. A multitude of people and vehicles obstructed my view, but I could see smoke and debris, some still sifting down from the sky. I thought it was probably a gas explosion.

Listening to the news reports that night accusations were made that the destruction at the church was not the result of a gas explosion or anything accidental, but instead a deliberate act. A bomb composed of 15 sticks of dynamite with a timer was the weapon, and of course, the timing, Sunday services, was not accidental. The intent was to kill and maim people. My mind reeled. I rationalized that it had to be someone, a maligned church member or a crazy guy who was angry. Who could ever intentionally cause such pain? My immediate response was, "Not me!"

The release of the names and photos of the four young girls who were killed and the 22 wounded preyed on my conscience, as did the news accounts detailing 21 prior bombings and numerous threats in Birmingham in the last eight years. The city, my new home that I had just learned to love, was called "Bombingham." Was I aware of this level of anger and violence? "Not me." Then, when I learned that the potential suspects were white men and the motive racism, my shame overwhelmed me. I searched my mind to see if I knew anyone capable of such violence, and the answer was immediate. "Not me!"

The 16th Street bombing awakened me to racial injustice in this country, but I didn't know what to do with this new-found knowledge. I wanted to talk about it with a Black peer, but did I do it? "Not me!" I had no Black peers as none were enrolled in my college and the Blacks I knew at home were from an older generation and I only saw them occasionally. I wanted to be able to understand by reading and listening to the media, but did I do it? "Not me!" I did put forth minimal effort but found the reporting contradictory and self-serving. It didn't seem relevant as I knew that I was not a violent person and had not been reared with negative feelings towards Blacks or any other group.

In the back of my mind, I still questioned. Did I do anything to encourage such hatred? My "Not me!" answer was more tenuous than before as my conscience niggled at my complacent state. I knew in my heart that I was not responsible, nor did I participate in or cause the violence leading up to this bombing; however, I could not in good conscience declare my innocence relative to the overall climate that fostered such radical racism.

My sin was not of commission, but the more subtle sin of omission.

I'm not exactly sure when I transitioned from a "Not me!" to a "Why not me?" attitude. I began to see beyond my own little, self-centered white world. Segregation now had meaning for me. I saw restricted work opportunities. I questioned why no Blacks were at my college. I thought about the lack of Blacks in my church and the restaurants I frequented. I looked at the political setting in Alabama that had few, if any, Blacks. I saw neighborhoods with no Blacks. The degree to which I accepted this situation as normal indicted me and negated the "Not me!" defense. I recognized that my ignorance and indifference helped foster a climate which other may have interpreted as acceptance of something I abhorred.

With my new-found knowledge and "Why not me?" attitude, I registered to vote. I sought, promoted, and voted for individuals who campaigned for racial justice. In my second year of teaching, a prime "Why not me?" opportunity presented itself when the school district requested volunteers to go to a formerly all Black school. I jumped at the chance. I was well received by my students and I loved them. Mentoring, tutoring, and community activism were also "Why not me?" opportunities I sought. Sitting in on teacher interviews, I approved Black candidates if at all possible. I found delightful new Black friends.

This "Why not me?" mentality continued throughout my 40 plus years in education, and in my personal life. My role in the Civil Rights struggle was as a witness more than anything else. I'm glad that timing was such that my mind was awakened to the African-American struggle, and I regret that my life existed in a vacuum before the Birmingham bombing. As horrific as that bombing was, it was a catalyst that changed me in a positive way. I no longer separate myself from issues that at first glance do not seem to pertain to me.

I am an old woman now and that terrible Sunday in Birmingham happened more than 50 years ago, but its impact on me is still fresh. I do see that inroads in racial justice have been made, but I also see echoes of the past on the nightly news. I pray that my country will stand strong against the temptation to repeat shameful behavior. We need sane, active voices to prevail; voices that do not yield to the "Not me," trap fostered either by choice or ignorance. Instead, this country needs citizens with a "Why not me?" attitude as we seek positive answers to today's complex social and political problems.

BOXERLESS BILL

In 1966, my future husband, Bill, began traveling the South selling a new product called a Salescaster. Salescasters were rectangular boxes about thirty-six inches long and six inches tall that could be mounted and used to communicate moving messages on safety, motivation, or production for many types of industry.

The size of the Huntsville sales market required a stay of several weeks, so Bill set up residence in a boarding house in the Five Points Historical Area. The lady who managed the boarding house only rented to single, young men, and was very particular about cleanliness, meal times, language, curfews, drinking, etc. The rooms were sparsely furnished with only twin beds and dressers. Bill and another man had a room on the second floor at the back of the house with a private entrance accessed by a steep, rather rickety wooden staircase.

Friendships developed among the young men of the boarding house as they played cards, swapped stories, and covered for each other when they fell short of their landlady's expectations. Bill's roommate ignored the house rules more than most of the young men. Having a steady girlfriend and the ease of an outside entrance, he was often not in by the established curfew. On those late nights, Bill left the screen door unlatched knowing that he would be in sooner or later. This plan worked well until one summer night in 1966.

Bam, bam, bam, Bill awoke abruptly to this loud noise, and his bed literally bouncing up and down across the floor. With a jolt, he sat up and found a huge, honey colored animal tied to his iron footboard. In his sleepy state, he was unsure whether it was a dog or a horse, where it came from, or why it was attached to his bed. What he did know was that that animal was after stray cats outside the house. When the caterwauling subsided, the animal, a big Great Dane dog, became friendly. He reared up on his hind legs with his feet on Bill's shoulders and this 200-pound dog looked him in the eyes. He had a collar and a tag, so it was obviously someone's pet. Bill also knew that when his roommate came home that dog would probably attack him, so he stayed up, played with the dog, and waited for his roommate for a while. Then he got sleepy and decided that he would tie the dog to his wrist so when his roommate came home he could control the dog. This was an excellent plan, but with some minor, unforeseen consequences.

It was about midnight when the commotion started. In the shadows, Bill could see the dog standing at attention near the foot of his bed and barking fast and furious. In his just awakened state, Bill did not respond quickly enough to the dog's barking to establish control of the dog or himself. Before he knew what was happening, he was on the floor being dragged toward the screen door as he heard his roommate's drunken voice at the bottom of the stairs.

In one bounding leap, this huge dog jumped through the bottom portion of the screen door, breaking the cross bars and ripping a gaping hole in the screen and pulling Bill off the bed. As the dog hit the landing outside the door, Bill tried to stop the forward motion of the dog by stretching his legs across the door facing. His attempts to stop the dog from dragging him through the door were thwarted by the hundreds of little sharp spines from the torn screen sticking and scratching him. When he attempted to move into a better position to stop the pain and gain control, the dog saw his chance and lunged down onto the steps. Of course, Bill followed, not voluntarily. All six feet of his backside were stretched out behind the dog with his arms leading, followed by his head bouncing down the stairs, and his legs and feet exiting last through the destroyed screen door.

The dog never stopped long enough for Bill to regain his footing. His roommate at the bottom of the stairs kept screaming for Bill to hold on to that dog. Lights came on in the houses around the boarding house. Bill was finally able to scream for his roommate to leave. When he left, the dog began to settle down. Bill tried to get to his feet, but this huge dog jumped up and knocked him flat on his back. The dog straddled him and licked his face. By now, a small crowd of people had gathered around this scene laughing hysterically. It was at that moment that Bill realized his boxer shorts were not with him but hung up on the bits of broken wire on the screen door. He wrestled the big dog off of him, attempted some effort at modesty, and ran back up the stairs with his bare bottom shining in the moonlight like new money. This time the Great Dane was the one who was being pulled involuntarily.

The next morning as he sat down at the breakfast table, Bill figured he was eating his last meal at the boarding house, certain that his landlady would throw him out. Everyone was smiling at him, making comments under their breaths, and waiting to see their landlady's reaction. No reaction came! It seemed that the little old lady was absolutely unaware that anything had happened. She was extremely hard of hearing and had removed her hearing aids before bed. In fact, she was pleased that "all her boys" were in such a good moods that morning. Bill, saved from eviction, repaired the screen, and continued to live in the boarding house for quite a while.

So, how did that Great Dane end up tied to Bill's bed? His roommate brought the dog home earlier that evening. He said he told Bill, but he must have been too asleep to comprehend. He tied the dog to his bed because he thought the dog, as strong as he was, could not move both Bill and the bed. The dog belonged to his girlfriend and they decided to leave him there while they went out drinking. Bill said he never figured out whether the dog was trying to attack his roommate or just happy to see him when he came home that night.

CORVETTE CHRISTMAS

Along about noon on a cold Christmas Eve, I settled back in my easy chair and prepared to escape the frenzy of kids, dogs, and relatives that infiltrated my home. I closed my eyes and set my breathing to a somewhat noisy, monotonous pace hoping that the brood would think I was asleep. As I slipped into a semi-conscious state, I allowed my mind to wander to my pride and joy, a red '67 Corvette Roadster convertible parked in my garage. Since it was not fully restored, I would have loved to slip outside and work on it for a couple of hours. However, I knew that if I exited the family room to work on my car the wife would silently label me Scrooge all the while contemplating the psychological damage being doing to the kids by not building family traditions. So, I sat in the easy chair like a prisoner of Christmas trapped by the sparkling lights, the smell of good food, and the clamor of the kids.

The last verse of *Jingle Bell*s roused me from this blissful state. I decided to show a token interest in the abundance of gifts under the tree. Several packages had my name prominently displayed, and I silently labeled each one in my mind. The candy cane striped package was probably after shave. The one all done up in Santa and elves paper was most likely a shirt or a sweater. That one might also contain a tie. Oh, how many of those types of things I've received over the years. I was not being ungrateful, just acknowledging the predictability of Christmas presents. I attempted to prepare myself emotionally for the required display of exuberance as evening approached and opening of family presents began.

My wife came into the living room where I was standing next to the tree. She told me that there was one more ornament for the tree, an ornament made especially for me, and placed it in my hand. Looking at the ornament, I saw that it was a round, shiny shell-like disc with a tiny red and white painted Corvette in the middle. Encircling the car the words *Corvette Christmas* and *1978* further piqued my attention. I turned and looked at my wife who was displaying a mischievous grin. As I found a place on the tree for the ornament, giggles, laughter and whispers filled the room. I realized that everyone was united in some kind of conspiracy relative to this ornament. I tried hard to repress a smile, but it crept across my face unconsciously. Searching my wife's face for answers, I only found a smug look and a twinkle in her eye so I sidled up to her with as much charm as I could muster and asked her what was meant by that ornament. Quickly, she twirled out of my arms and told me that for at least the rest of the afternoon I would feel about Christmas as I had when I was a little boy.

Well, I must admit that the old stoicism for which I was famous slipped into a mild surge of anticipation as I viewed those colorful packages again. I found myself trying to talk everyone into opening presents before dinner. Even the kids were against me on that point. During the remainder of that long afternoon, my wife became a real name dropper as she rattled off names of 'Vette catalogues that I used to replace parts on my car. These names were simply not in her vocabulary and only fueled my desire to rip open those packages. Once she mentioned my '64 Vette in the garage and I almost went into cardiac arrest thinking she had ordered parts for the wrong car, but upon seeing my distress she quickly clarified that my 'Vette was a '67.

Now in order to fully appreciate this situation you must realize that my wife never acknowledged that my 'Vette was anything more than a used car. She was a good sport about my cars. I remember one time she stood with me in the pouring rain in Bowling Green, Kentucky just to get a first glimpse of the new 'Vette. My love of Corvettes was accepted, but she was simply lukewarm regarding any car.

The afternoon slowly wound down and Christmas Eve officially arrived after candlelight services. Dinner was served and kids were readied for bed. I built a roaring fire and at last, the timing and ambiance was perfect to open presents. My four-year-old played Santa and brought me the first package as she thought she could be more patient than me. Then one at a time, I began to unwrap that multitude of packages and nowhere was there a shirt, tie, sweater or after shave. A treasure of Corvette things awaited me. Books, magazines subscriptions, dealer models, jacket, calendars, and even an owner's manual for my car were just some of the gifts I received. As I sat in the middle of the floor with those gifts spread out all around me, I realized, for just a moment, that I was a kid again. That old magic and excitement of Christmas made a return visit to me that night thanks to my wife's love. Now, I find I can answer an age-old question. Yes, Bill, there is a Santa and she sleeps under my covers every night.

THE GIFT OF A SONG

For almost a year my precious daughter was unable to sing. The musical void she left in our church was quite noticeable as she was often called to do scheduled solos, as well as last minute replacement solos when others were unable to perform. Also, she sang weekly on the praise team. Church members were concerned with her absence and I was frequently asked when she would sing again. I reluctantly told people I didn't know when or if she would ever find her voice for singing in church again.

My daughter was just thirteen when she witnessed her father die very suddenly from a massive coronary. Thirteen is such a tender age for a girl to lose a beloved and wonderful father. The grief and anger was palatable and found its way into all aspects of her life. A happy, outgoing child became sullen and isolated. She was unable to talk about his death and so internalized her feelings to the point that she didn't want anyone to talk about his passing. Efforts at counseling, either lay or professional, did not afford relief. I didn't know whether she was angry with God or with me for failing to keep him alive, but I became more and more concerned as her voice stilled.

This child was very musical. She basically taught herself to play the piano and accompanied herself as she sang. She won state awards for her talent and was frequently asked to sing at weddings and funerals. It was such a joy for me to listen as she

138

prepared her music for Sunday services. She often spent hours practicing her selection. I knew a lot of the joy had gone out of her life and I was so afraid that music had gone with it. I tried not to question too much. I knew she would talk about it when she could.

Christmas 1989 would be hard on both of us as it was almost a year after his death. I was surprised when my daughter announced that she had found a song that she wanted to sing in church. It was a new Amy Grant song, *Heirlooms*. I heard the tape playing as she practiced in her room, but I could not understand the words.

It was the last Sunday night in church before we were scheduled to go home to Alabama for Christmas. She was to sing. As she stepped up to the mike, I heard a slight mumble from the congregation and several turned to smile at me. A friend sitting next to me reached over and touched my hand. My daughter looked so confident as she began. The song started off very softly and I strained to hear the words. The church was so quiet you could hear a pin drop. Then she moved confidently into the old performing personality with clear enunciation and vocal display.

The first verse finished, and I knew my daughter was on her way back from that terrible, dark sadness. Then the next verse finished and my heart settled down. And finally, the last line of the song, where our precious Father is acknowledged as real, not an heirloom, took on a combined meaning. She sang in a manner that conveyed that her earthly father and her heavenly Father were not just heirlooms. With a depth of expression I have rarely heard she completed the song. Everyone knew she was singing not only about her heavenly Father, but her own father who was in heaven. There was total silence after the song and then, a thunderous standing ovation. I noticed many members of the congregation wiping their eyes. The preacher got up to begin the sermon, and he, too, was obviously moved by her. After a few moments he thanked her for her gift of song and said that both her father in heaven and her heavenly Father were pleased with her performance and her praise. From all around me people were hugging me.

I knew we had passed a milestone in the grief process, not that the process was complete. It would rear its ugly head time and time again for both of us, but that song that night was a gift of hope for me that my child would survive this terrible ordeal with her faith in God intact and her gift of song set free. I think she found the strength in the words and sentiment of Amy Grant's beautiful song that freed her to live once again.

"PUTTIN' IT ALL ON THE LINE"

All of my life I have heard the phrase, "Put it all on the line." It meant doing whatever you had to do to accomplish your goal. I never realized that phrase had such a literal meaning for me until a few years ago.

I was sitting with my frail, 88-year-old, wheelchair bound Dad at the kitchen table feeding him breakfast. I mechanically wiped the spilled milk dribbling from his chin and the cereal with the little Os from his face and clothes. I scooped the remaining cereal and banana bits to the side of the bowl nearest him so he could find the last bites. This was our routine now. He was mostly immobile due to contractures from Parkinson's disease and reduced oxygenation from lungs damaged by years of breathing in lint from his textile mill work. Dad did not usually talk during breakfast as it took too much energy, but I filled that empty void with meaningless words. It was my way of trying to hold on to him even though it was obvious that he was slipping away a little more each day.

At one point during breakfast, I saw him staring out the back-screen door. The main door was open as it was a pretty spring day. He stopped with spoon midway between the bowl and his mouth. I asked him what he saw. Thinking it might have been an early robin or the redbud tree with its startling pink blooms against a bare landscape, I shifted my gaze to match his. I saw nothing extraordinary. Then, he looked at me with eyes as clear as I had seen in days, and stated those poles saw us through some difficult financial times. I was taken aback, unsure whether he was lucid or fantasizing as he was prone to do in his later years, or even what poles he meant. I started questioning to ascertain his state of mind. His answers were appropriate, and he began to tell me the story of his clothesline pole business.

His clothesline pole business started the year before I began college, 1963. The old cotton mill where he worked for many, many years was disposing of some used, unneeded steel pipes. Those pipes were about twelve feet long and four to five inches in diameter. Dad asked and they gave him the pipes if he would dispose of them which meant they were free. Every day he brought pipes home and stacked them in the backyard.

On his days off and using his blow torch, he turned these pipes into unbelievably durable clothesline poles. He cut each pole into two pieces. One piece was eight feet long and the other piece was four feet long. Then he cut a hole in the middle of the shorter piece and welded the long piece inside. Next, he drilled three holes for wires on the cross member. He told me that he made two poles before he went to work every day in the morning as he worked the night shift starting at 10 p.m. He sold the clothesline poles for ten dollars a pair installed.

Dad got quiet, and since I wanted desperately to keep him talking I asked him how many clothesline poles he sold. He smiled and told me to just look around Huntsville and see those poles at many, many houses. Word of mouth was his advertising.

Then a revelation came out of his mouth that stunned me. He told me those clothesline poles paid for my college. I knew that Mother scrimped and saved on groceries to send me an occasional five dollars spending money, but I never questioned how they financed tuition, housing, and books. Now, to hear that the money came from building and installing clothesline poles shocked me, but I was always in awe of my dad's entrepreneurship. Of course, back in the early 1960s, the cost of college was in the hundreds of dollars rather than the thousands of today. Dad said he made the poles the entire time I was in college, so my expenses were paid for by the poles, ten dollars at a time.

As I sat there pondering this revelation, Dad's lucidity retreated. It left as quickly as it came. No longer would he talk to me about the poles or finish his breakfast, but I came away with a new appreciation for my parents and the sacrifices they made to send me to college. I also felt guilty knowing that I had not sacrificed for my own education nearly as much as they did.

Later as I was walking back to my house across the street, I noticed those nondescript metal clothesline poles in almost every yard, and marveled that they were in as good a condition as when they were installed some 50 years ago. Those previously mundane poles took on a new meaning, symbolizing the sacrifice and love of my parents. At the same time, I wondered how many other wonderful stories of my parents' love for their family were lost. I was so glad Dad was able to share this one with me.

ABOUT THE AUTHOR

Theresa Hanvey Fallwell, originally from Madison County, Alabama, is currently a retired teacher living in Katy, Texas. She enjoys writing and finds inspiration in the people and places of her youth. As a teacher of more than 40 years, she first started story writing to pique her students' interest and practice specific comprehension skills. From there she progressed to grant writing and curriculum development for the U.S. Department of Education. She has received numerous awards for writing and teaching including runner up to the Texas Elementary Teacher of the Year Award.

Mrs. Fallwell is mother to Gwen and Patrick and grandmother to Bryce, Abbey, Claire, Christie, and several dogs. When she is not doing grandma duties, she loves to quilt, take long walks, read good books, cook, and do genealogy work. Her favorite activity is to return to Alabama to rekindle old relationships and experience the very visceral reaction produced by the absolute beauty of the area she calls home, despite being gone for more than fifty years.

Made in the USA
Lexington, KY
01 August 2018